1997 £12

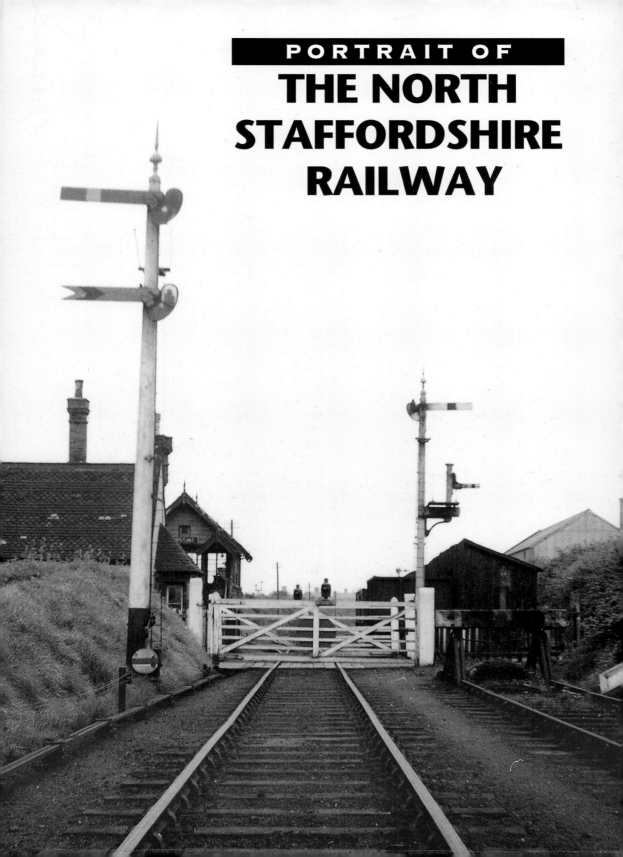

PORTRAIT OF
THE NORTH STAFFORDSHIRE RAILWAY

PORTRAIT OF
THE NORTH STAFFORDSHIRE RAILWAY

Rex Christiansen

IAN ALLAN
Publishing

First published 1997

ISBN 0 7110 2546 0

© Ian Allan Ltd 1997

Published by Ian Allan Publishing

an imprint of Ian Allan Ltd, Terminal House, Station Approach, Shepperton, Surrey TW17 8AS.
Printed by Ian Allan Printing Ltd at its works at Coombelands in Runnymede, England.

Code: 9710/B1

Front cover: The NSR shared Manchester London Road station with the LNWR and GCR. NSR No 120 was built by Beyer Peacock in 1874. The class survived Grouping by several years until the LMS withdrew them between 1927-33. *Ian Allan Library (IAL)/Bucknall Collection*

Back cover, top: As NSR No 87 departs from Stoke station the fireman checks that all is well. *IAL/Bucknall Collection*

Back cover, bottom: A classic scene at Macclesfield station in 1910 as NSR No 88 runs through the middle road. *IAL/Bucknall Collection*

Below: Ex-NSR tank No 2 shunting at Mossley Common Colliery, in January 1962. The locomotive was one of four sold by the LMS to Manchester Collieries in 1937. It was restored to its NSR livery at Crewe Works as part of Stoke Golden Jubilee celebrations in 1960 and is now preserved. *J. R. Carter*

Bibliography

Atterbury, P.; *AA Discovering Britain's Lost Railways*
Baker, A. C.; *The Cheadle Railway*
Baker, A. C.; *The Potteries Loop Line: An Illustrated History*
Baker, A. & Morrison, G.; *Crewe Sheds*
Butt, R. J. V.; *The Directory of Railway Stations*
Christiansen, R.; *Forgotten Railways: The West Midlands*
Christiansen, R.; *Rail Centres: Crewe*
Christiansen, R.; *Regional History of Railways: The West Midlands*
Christiansen R. & Miller, R. W.; *The North Staffordshire Railway*
Daniels G., & Dench, L. A.; *Passengers No More*
Dow, G.; *North Staffordshire Album*
Jeuda, B.; *The Macclesfield, Bollington & Marple Railway*
Jeuda, B.; *North Staffordshire Railway*
Jeuda, B., 'The Knotty': *An Illustrated Survey of the North Staffordshire Railway*
Jones, P.; *The Stafford & Uttoxeter Railway*
Keys, R.; *The Churnet Valley Railway*
Lester, C. R.; *The Stoke to Market Drayton Line*
Lewthwaite, G. C.; *Branch Line Index*
'Manifold'; *The North Staffordshire Railway: A History of the Line and its Locomotives*
'Manifold'; *The Leek & Manifold Valley Light Railway*
Nock, O. S.; *Britain's New Railway*
Reed, M. C.; *The London & North Western Railway*
Signalling Record Society; *British Railways Layout Plans of the 1950s: ex-North Staffordshire Railway Lines*
Turner, K.; *The Leek & Manifold Valley Light Railway*
Yonge, J. & Jacobs, G.; *London Midland Region Track Diagrams*

Also consulted:

NSR Board minutes in BRB Historical Records Office
Journals and magazines of the Branch Line Society, Manchester. Locomotive Society, Railway & Canal Historical Society
Hollick, J.R.; *The Workings of the Locomotives and Trains of Private Firms over the North Staffordshire Railway.* (Typescript paper c1958)
Notes for railtours of the Branch Line Society, British Rail, The Institution of Mining Engineers
Bradshaw's Shareholders Guides and timetables; timetables of Great Central, Great Western, London & North Western and North Staffordshire railways

Contents

Acknowledgements

The number of books about the North Staffordshire Railway constantly being added to my library shelves is testimony to the affection in which this comparatively small railway is still held, nearly three-quarters of a century after it lost its identity at Grouping in 1923. I have had far more books to draw on as sources of reference than when I wrote *The North Staffordshire Railway* with my friend, R. W. (Bob) Miller, now Chairman of the Manchester Locomotive Society, more than a quarter of a century ago.

While Bob Miller has read the manuscript and provided some of the illustrations, responsibility for the content is wholly mine. I am also grateful to a number of people for extra historical material, including Harold Forster MBE, the late Dr Jack Hollick, Hugh B. Oliver, Ron Owen, Nigel Payton, Richard Price and Jeffrey Williams.

Encouragement for this book, written at the suggestion of the publishers, has come from a number of people, not least fellow members of the Railway & Canal Historical Society.

Rex Christiansen
Chelford, Cheshire 1997

Note — the photographs
Many of the illustrations in this book are taken from rare historic prints; in some cases the print is unique and it is often the case that the negative has long vanished. For this reason a number of illustrations which would normally be excluded, due to indifferent quality, are published here because of their historic importance.

The station diagrams are simplified versions of maps published by the Signalling Record Society and compiled by John Swift with permission from the compiler.

Photographic credits
Most of the illustrations come from collections; some titles are abbreviated in the picture credits. The full details are:

LPC	Locomotive Publishing Company
LGRP	Locomotive & General Railway Photographs
IAL/Bucknall Coll	The Bucknall Collection in the Ian Allan Library
HMRS	Historical Model Railway Society Collection

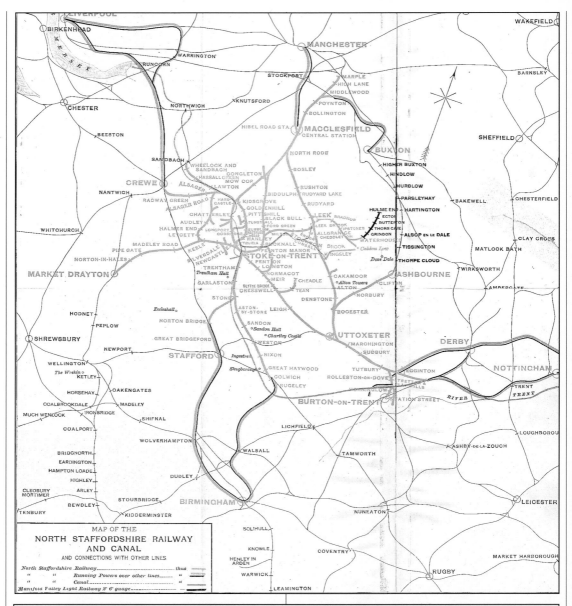

Above: Official NSR map. Undated, but probably Edwardian as it shows the Leek & Manifold Light Railway, opened in 1905, but not the Trentham Park branch of 1910. The Trent & Mersey Canal and Caldon Canal (between Etruria and Leek) are in (now faded) light blue. The Leek & Manifold is an example of curious emphasis placed by the company on its different lines, for while that is identified by a thick black line, the LNWR main line north and south of its junctions with the NSR at Norton Bridge and Colwich is given a thin line rating. The extensive NSR running powers are shown, with the exception of Crewe-Chester-North Wales, used by the summer Llandudno expresses, possibly because they were introduced after the map was issued. The square format embracing lines from Leeds to the Severn Valley suggests the NSR system was superimposed on a standard commercial railway map of the period. *Author's collection*

The 'Knotty' is Born

Once, when I visited the late Dr J. R. Hollick at his home in Ashbourne with R. W. 'Bob' Miller (with whom I wrote a history of the North Staffordshire Railway) afternoon tea was halted. We went upstairs because 'the afternoon train had to be run through the valley' on his model of the Leek & Manifold Valley Light Railway.

'Dr Jack' was one of a group of highly knowledgeable historians and enthusiasts called 'Manifold', who kept alive the memory of the 'Knotty' in the early 1950s, when it was in danger of being forgotten. Their history is now a classic.

They remembered the Knotty with affection, for its trains 'were the first trains they loved as children,' and they felt, 'it was one of the finest railways in Britain. Never afraid of a foe, however big, if its cause was just. The railway might well have taken the Staffordshire Terrier as its crest, for it was a veritable terrier among railways, true to those it served and jealous of its rights.'

Railwaymen always knew the company as the Knotty, because its emblem was the distinctive Staffordshire Knot. Many of the smaller pre-Grouping companies had nicknames, which were often derogatory — like 'slow and dirty' for the Somerset & Dorset Railway — but the North Staffordshire's was affectionate.

It was efficient, profitable and enterprising, as it demonstrated from its formation, when in 1846 it became the largest canal-owning railway by amalgamating with the Trent & Mersey. In that way it developed, rather than destroyed, the Potteries' main transport artery. The 119-mile canal carried more than a quarter of a million tons

Below: When the LNWR and NSR agreed to work some Euston-Manchester (London Road) expresses through the Potteries rather than Crewe, they became the smaller company's most prestigious services. Class G 4-4-0 No 87 departs from Stoke with a train of mixed LNWR stock. Note the water column on platform end with luggage trolleys parked nearby. *IAL*

Above: Another close liaison with the LNWR developed when the NSR introduced summer expresses between Derby and the North Wales coast resorts. Class G 4-4-0 No 86 makes a spirited departure from Stoke with a Derby-Llandudno express in 1910, the year it was built at Stoke. The first coach is an NSR tricomposite from Burton upon Trent, with two GNR coaches from Grantham behind. *Author's collection*

Below: The NSR was noted for having three gauges. Two of the gauges were seen on the 2ft 6in Leek & Manifold Valley Light Railway, running through outstanding scenery between Waterhouses and Hulme End in the hills of the Staffordshire/Derbyshire border. Its rolling stock included bogie transporter wagons which carried standard gauge NSR stock. The L&MVLR was owned by a separate company but was worked by the NSR. It is remembered for the two locomotives with ballroom-proportioned cabs and coaches of equal spaciousness. *LGRP*

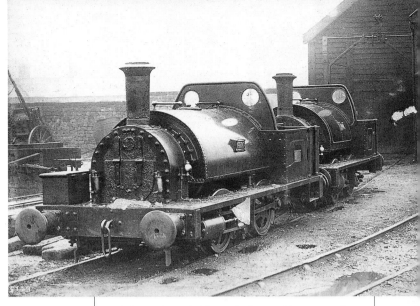

Right: The Caldon Low quarries used the third gauge. A 3ft 6in system worked by three 0-4-0 tanks: *Toad* and *Frog*, built by Henry Hughes of Loughborough in 1877 and joined by *Bobs* — an 'almost local' product from the Stafford works of W. G. Bagnall — in 1901. *LPC*

of goods and minerals every year after its construction between 1766 and 1804.

Having made canal history, the NSR became a company without delusions of grandeur, yet tough enough to beat competition from the far bigger railway companies which surrounded it.

As it asserted in the *Railway Year Book*: 'There is probably not another British railway of the size and importance of the NSR that is so little known in London. This is accounted for by the fact that the NSR is purely a local line, although NSR milk vans can be seen on the passenger trains of the GN (Great Northern) and other railways. Jointly with the LNWR, the NSR works through traffic via Stoke between Euston and Manchester.'

The Macclesfield-Stoke-Colwich route, 25kV electrified in the 1960s, remains the shortest between London and Manchester, five miles less than the West Coast main line via Crewe, which passes to the west of the Potteries.

The NSR was a line of three gauges. Besides the standard, there was the 2ft 6in of the Leek & Manifold Valley and a small 3ft 6in gauge system in Caldon limestone quarries. The NSR, as I shall generally call it, because constant references to the Knotty would be rather too gushing, was notable for the speed at which it was built. Within a few years of its formation in 1845, it had opened 111 miles — almost half the total with which it became an important constituent of the LMS, rated sixth by number of locomotives and seventh in mileage.

The NSR was far more profitable for its shareholders — 7,925 in 1913, one of the golden years of steam railways — than many other railway companies. It was notable for the way it developed good relations with its neighbours, partly because its routes were too strategic for them to ignore,

and through exploiting relations with companies with which it negotiated more than 300 miles of running powers.

The way it got people from the densely-populated Potteries to the nearest seaside resorts along the North Wales coast was classic enterprise, which included building its own locomotives, with tenders of sufficient capacity for the round trip to Llandudno, to avoid buying LNWR coal.

The NSR successfully mastered problems caused by the diverse nature of the areas it served. At its heart lay the industrial Potteries and yet only a few miles away were areas of sparsely populated countryside, whose praises it sang in a pocket-sized 'Official Illustrated Guide' of 150 pages. That was too dull a title for its publicity department, which re-titled it *Picturesque Staffordshire*. The main idea, stated the preface, was to dispel the notion held by many people that Staffordshire was a 'bleak and stony county'.

After Grouping, the LMS began branch closures and British Rail and Dr Beeching compounded them. Much has been destroyed, yet much remains, notably at Stoke station and the square outside.

Those who knew the Knotty retained strong memories for years. The Rev Noel Benham, who first saw its trains running on the Stone-Colwich main line across the valley from Yarlet Prep School, recalled that during World War 1, soldiers often went up to the front in France packed in coaches belonging to various pre-Grouping companies. All were painted grey and their company symbols removed, yet he felt at home among those of the NSR, which he identified by the company initials on leather window straps.

9

Above: Handling Euston expresses between Manchester and Stoke was well within the capabilities of a number of classes of NSR locomotives, including sturdy tanks, although banking was required from Macclesfield. 0-6-4T No 119, built at Stoke in 1918 and in immaculate condition, prepares to depart from London Road station with a Euston express made up of LNWR stock. *IAL/Bucknall Collection*

Below: Several classes of NSR locomotives worked regularly into Manchester (London Road), including neat 2-4-0s like No 19, built at Stoke in 1872. It is seen after renewal in 1905, which gave it 15 more years of life before scrapping. The locomotive was turned-out slightly cleaner than its tender. *IAL/Bucknall Collection*

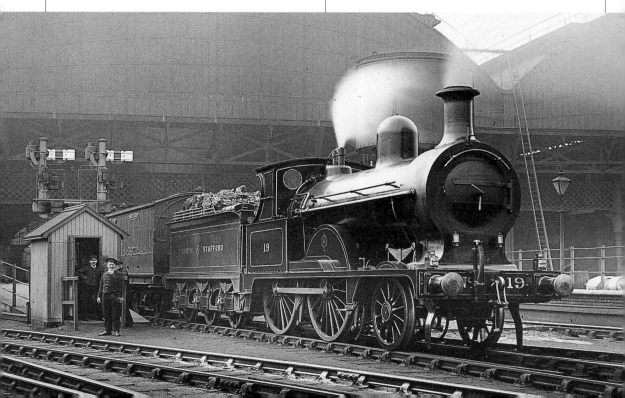

Main Lines

'The North Staffordshire Railway binds together the range of Pottery towns, like a thread stringing beads.' So stated George Measom's *Official Illustrated Guide to the LNWR* in 1861. But the NSR did a lot more that, having earned an immediate place in history when the eight lines which formed its backbone were authorised on 26 June 1846 without Parliamentary opposition.

There were to be four connections with the infant London & North Western Railway and another to the Midland Railway.

The embryo system was scissor-shaped. A main line continuing south from the Macclesfield branch of the Manchester & Birmingham, through Stoke to Colwich, with a branch from Stone to Norton Bridge, formed one blade; Crewe-Stoke-Derby formed the other. There were also branches from Stoke to Newcastle-under-Lyme and neighbouring Silverdale; from Lawton Junction, Alsager, to the LNWR at Sandbach; and a secondary route from North Rode, near Congleton, to Uttoxeter, through Leek and the mainly rural Churnet Valley lying to the east of the Potteries.

Measom included a North Staffordshire Line section in his guide because 'several of the London trains for Manchester leave the Trent Valley at Colwich station and run through the Potteries to Macclesfield. The principal towns on this line are Stoke-upon-Trent (*sic*), Congleton and Macclesfield.'

Capital created for construction of the Pottery Line totalled £1½ million — just over half that authorised for the eight original lines. The Pottery Line Act also vested the Trent & Mersey Canal in the NSR. Each of the original Acts laid down a completion time of seven years and there were

Below: A reminder that the NSR was not the only company besides the LNWR at London Road station is provided by the background to NSR No 120 blowing off before departure: in an adjacent platform is a Great Central tank locomotive. No 120 was one of a batch of six Class E 0-6-0s built by Beyer Peacock in 1874, which survived Grouping by several years until the LMS withdrew them between 1927-33.
IAL/Bucknall Collection

detailed safeguards regarding junctions with other companies.

There was immediate financial stringency, the Pottery Line Act stating that if the branch from Stoke to Newcastle was not opened within a year of the main line, it would be illegal for the NSR to pay an ordinary dividend until it was complete.

There was a public holiday throughout the Potteries when the first sod of the NSR was cut in a field at Stoke in September 1846, at a ceremony marred by the buckling of the silver spade used by the Chairman, John Ricardo, the local MP.

The scale and speed of the enterprise by the young and comparatively small company was evident from the start. It began changing the face of the landscape by placing contracts for 77 miles of railway: including Macclesfield-Colwich and Norton Bridge (47 miles), Stoke-Uttoxeter (16½ miles) and the Newcastle-under-Lyme, Crewe and Sandbach branches.

The biggest contract went to Thomas Brassey and included a number of major works. Brassey had to follow the canal builders and tunnel through the Trent and Mersey watershed at Harecastle. Three tunnels were bored, of which the longest was a mile. The tunnels were separated by deep cuttings. The most spectacular engineering works were two high viaducts across

river valleys near Congleton. Both were built with brick spans. The longer, North Rode, was 1,255ft. It had 20 arches and a maximum height of 106ft.

The route, surveyed by George Stephenson, was magnificent and despite the hilly Pennine flanks south of Macclesfield, the ruling gradient was no stiffer than 1 in 330, although a two-mile bank at 1 in 102 was needed to lift the line out of Macclesfield. It was, wrote O. S. Nock in *Britain's New Railway* (about electrification in the 1960s), 'a notably good alignment which was subsequently used for some very smartly-timed passenger services'.

Stoke was placed on the railway map of Britain with the opening, on 17 April 1848, of the first stretch of the NSR, formed by an 11-mile branch from the LNWR at Norton Bridge in the countryside five miles north of Stafford. The NSR had to be content with a temporary station at Norton Bridge, until settlement of a two-year dispute with the LNWR allowed a junction to be established. The original NSR terminus at Whieldon Grove, Stoke, was also temporary.

But Stoke quickly became the hub of the system and the NSR built a through station of great dignity. It was the centrepiece of a square completed by matching workers' houses on either side and a three-storey hotel, with 130 bedrooms

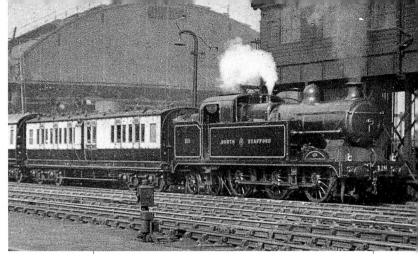

Below left: Outside London Road station, NSR Class B 2-4-0T No 28 stands coupled to an unidentified LNWR locomotive, possibly as pilot of a Euston express. LNWR 0-6-2T No 1199 is on an adjacent line, masking the well-loaded tender of an unidentified 4-6-0. *IAL/Bucknall Collection*

Above right: Class F 0-6-4T No 118 about to depart from London Road station with the 12.5pm Euston express shortly after the end of World War 1. *R. W. Miller Collection*

Centre right: A Manchester-Stoke all-stations train of late Victorian years at Prestbury, near Macclesfield, headed by Class B 2-4-0T No 18, carrying express code headlamps. The train, photographed in the mid-1880s, is made up of LNWR four-wheel compartment coaches. *IAL/Bucknall Collection*

Below: Manchester-Stoke local services were often worked by 2-4-0s. No 38, one of two Class C locomotives, built at Stoke in 1874 and withdrawn in 1912, heads a train of LNWR six-wheel compartment stock. No 38 has a tender with outside springs. A platelayer's four-wheel trolley is in the left foreground. *IAL/Bucknall Collection*

Left: A classic NSR scene from the Bucknall Collection: passengers on Macclesfield Central down platform (left) and a railway worker standing beside the water column on the up, watch the heavy 12.5pm Manchester-Euston express of mixed LNWR carriages storm through the middle road. Class H 0-6-0 No 88 was built at Stoke in 1909, a year before.
IAL/Bucknall Collection

Below left: Double-framed 0-6-0 No 85 (Neilson, 1885) on the up through line at Macclesfield Central on 28 June 1902. It was among a batch of six locomotives which formed NSR Class F. They remained in service until 1909-13. The signal in the background is the Hibel Road distant: a reminder of the short distance between Macclesfield Central and Hibel Road stations.
Ken Nunn Collection, LCGB

Above right: The early Nationalisation (1952) scene at North Rode, a three-storey rural station five miles south of Macclesfield Hibel Road station. It was at the junction of the Stoke and Churnet Valley lines and although services via Leek were withdrawn in November 1960, North Rode remained open to passengers until May 1962, when it was closed and later demolished as a prelude to 25kV electrification through the Potteries. *LGRP*

Centre right: Congleton, a small but busy town, eight miles south of Macclesfield and 12 miles north of Stoke, had a station dominated by a tall signalbox beside a level crossing. The box gave the signalman a clear view over the station roof. An NSR guide of 1908 noted that 'handsome villas' had been erected on a steep half-mile road between town and station. The picture is dated 1948. *LGRP*

Bottom right: Longport's two distinctive platform canopies survived into BR days. In 1952, the ageing gates of the level crossing were in need of paint. *LGRP*

and ample stabling, facing the Jacobean-style station frontage. All are preserved.

The next section completed was Stoke-Uttoxeter (16 miles), opened on 7 August 1848, followed by Uttoxeter-Burton Junction (12½ miles) on 11 September. Stoke-Crewe (14½ miles) and Harecastle (later Kidsgrove)-Congleton (5½ miles) both opened on 9 October, together with Stoke's permanent station.

Disputes with large and influential landowners led to construction delays at both ends of the Crewe-Derby route, which established a through link between Northwest England, North Wales and Eastern England. Lord Crewe forced the company to make a three-mile deviation near his seat at Crewe Hall, on the eastern outskirts of the town. The 8½-mile line from Harecastle joined the LNWR line into Crewe just south of the station.

Some years later the LNWR contemptuously dismissed the route's value, one of its guide books describing it as 'a short branch constructed to accommodate the salt traffic of Cheshire'. But it was far more important than that, for it gave the expanding railway town a short and direct link with its nearest coalfield in North Staffordshire.

The Crewe branch gained another connection when the LNWR developed Basford Hall marshalling yards and built a sharply curved and heavily graded spur for goods traffic. After burrowing under the West Coast main line, it climbed into the yards in a south-facing direction.

The Eastern England link was completed by a 4½-mile section between Marston and the Midland's Derby-Birmingham main line at Willington Junction, five miles short of Derby. The section was authorised by one of the NSR original Acts, but construction was delayed by Sir Henry Every. Long negotiations and two applications to Parliament took place before the route was agreed. It opened on 18 June 1849 — the same day as the Churnet Valley. The NSR used running powers to reach Derby.

The Macclesfield-Colwich route was completed in two stages in 1849: the 11½ miles south from Stone to Colwich opened on 1 May and Congleton-Macclesfield (8½ miles) on 18 June. The main line joined the LNWR at Hibel Road station, Macclesfield, 17½ miles from Manchester London Road station. There was an NSR engine shed and goods yard north of the station but the NSR had to use running powers to reach them. Hibel Road was a joint station just north of the present station, then called Central and solely owned by the NSR.

Although the NSR reached Macclesfield, an ever growing town with an important silk industry, four years after the Manchester & Birmingham, it was more heartily welcomed by residents. A local historian, C. Stella Davies, thought it was because by the time the NSR arrived, people no longer feared travelling in trains at high speeds.

Completion between Stone and Colwich had been delayed. There had been discussions about opening the section almost a year earlier, but the consulting engineer, George Bidder, reported that it had been 'retarded according to the instructions of the directors'.

It ran through almost empty countryside but this did not deter the building of highly ornate village stations. The area remains a pleasant green belt separating the Potteries from the West Midlands.

Below left: No 45, one of Adams'
handsome Class K 4-4-2Ts of
1911-12, passes Etruria gasworks
with the 7.30am Derby-Manchester
London Road on 9 June 1919. It was
booked to take 150min for 83 miles.
Ken Nunn Collection LCGB

Above right: Etruria — with 2-4-0T
No 48 on (probably) a Macclesfield
train of brown and white painted
coaches. The tall signal post carries
the up main starter, with the up relief
line distant for Cliff Vale on a
bracket. Signals on the right control
the down main and relief lines.
R. W. Miller Collection

Centre right: Stoke station was
improved through the years but
never substantially extended. A view
looking north, after completion in
1894 of a single-span roof of 85ft,
replacing the original three-span
roof. The station was lit by gas and
also electricity, then a new wonder.
The supply was fed from the
company's own power station built
underground next to the southern
passenger subway. *LGRP*

Below: The Bucknall Collection
contains several photographs of
NSR tank locomotives at Stoke
hauling LNWR stock. Class M
0-4-4T No 42 awaits departure with
a train headed by a second class
brake, in about 1910. The
locomotive, Stoke built, was then
about two years old.
IAL/Bucknall Collection

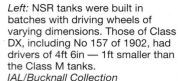

Left: NSR tanks were built in batches with driving wheels of varying dimensions. Those of Class DX, including No 157 of 1902, had drivers of 4ft 6in — 1ft smaller than the Class M tanks. *IAL/Bucknall Collection*

Centre left: NSR No 1 was an 0-6-2T of the 'New L' class. It was built at Stoke in 1923, the year after the class was introduced. *IAL/Bucknall Collection*

Below: Stone station of 1848 was the work of H. A. Hunt, the architect of Stoke station, also of Jacobean-style design. The Colwich up and down platforms (left in this 1952 scene) were demolished during electrification. The other platforms have an EMU local service and Stone-Norton Bridge is used by Manchester-Birmingham expresses. *Ian Allan Library*

Above right: Trentham was among the architectural gems of British, rather than solely NSR, stations. It was built for the Duke of Sutherland's Trentham Hall estate and had, as George Dow noted in his *North Staffordshire Album*, 'a Mediterranean air about it'. 'Royal Scot' 4-6-0 No 6169 *The Boy Scout* heads a Manchester-Euston express in August 1957. *Ian Allan Library*

Below right: Barlaston & Tittensor was named Barlaston in 1972 and remains one of three intermediate stations for local trains between Stoke and Norton Bridge. *LGRP*

19

Above: The original wooden building at Fenton station was closed in November 1906 and replaced by a more substantial one nearby on the following day. Standing beside the gates (left) is porter Jack Martin. The second Fenton station closed in 1961. *Hugh B. Oliver Collection*

Left: The Stoke-Derby line squeezed through the heart of Longton, where, c1907, a Class D 0-6-0T heads an up Loop line service. The signal post was reputed to be the second highest on the NSR. The station retained its overall roof until 1941. An indicator clock (bottom left) shows the next down service was due to depart at 10.32am. *Hugh B. Oliver Collection*

PORTRAIT OF THE NORTH STAFFORDSHIRE RAILWAY   INDEX

Standing Order Mandate

Please use ink and BLOCK CAPITALS

To

....Bank

Address of bank ....

....Post Code......................

Account Name...

Account Number ....Sort Code.........-.........-......

Please pay to Royal Bank of Scotland, 50 Bramhall Lane South, Bramhall, Stockport, SK7 1AJ. Sort Code 16-14-20 Account Number 11382648

The sum of £ .... on the ....day of.............................

200..... and (*annually / quarterly / monthly) thereafter (*on the same date for

.... years / until further notice.) *delete as applicable.

Signed ....

Name ....

Address ....

....Post Code........................

Please return completed forms to
Cllr Patsy Calton, FREEPOST NWW14172, Stockport, SK7 1YE.
No stamp required.

Right: Cresswell became a junction when the Cheadle Railway opened to goods in 1888. The branch had a passenger service between 1901 and 1963 and Cresswell was used by Crewe-Derby trains until November 1966. Cresswell was also incorporated into the Loop line timetable. In Edwardian days, the first service was the 5.23am 'Rail Motor Car' to Stoke, where passengers had to wait 4min for a connection to Tunstall. *LGRP*

Centre right: Leigh, about 1890, with a Uttoxeter-bound train headed by 2-4-0T No 9, built at Stoke in 1874 for the opening of the Loop line. The train consists of a typical Loop line formation of close-coupled, four-wheel NSR coaches.
Dr J. R. Hollick Collection

Below: Uttoxeter, 1890. 2-4-0 No 39 with a Derby-Stoke all-stations service. A rake of four- and six-wheel coaches has several vans attached at the rear. A shunter and his horse stand by a milk van (left). Churnet Valley and Ashbourne trains used the curved platforms spanned by the covered over-bridge. Uttoxeter declined in importance after the withdrawal of regular passenger services over the former Great Northern Stafford & Uttoxeter route in 1939 and of Churnet Valley services to Macclesfield in winter 1960. *LGRP*

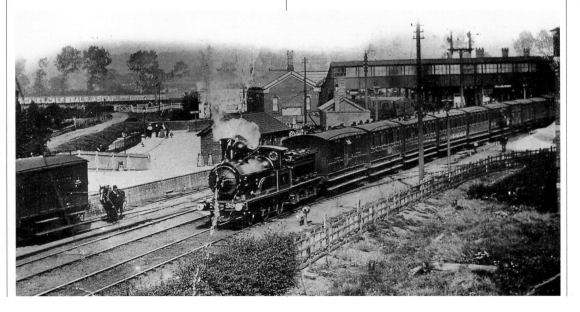

Left: Sudbury in Edwardian days: a substantial station building with ornate roof tiles and chimneys. Milk cans stand on both platforms. Sudbury was among several stations between Crewe and Derby closed to passengers in November 1966. *Author's collection*

Centre left: Tutbury — where railways retreated and returned! As a junction for the NSR Burton upon Trent branch, the substantial station was flanked by a small marshalling yard and goods sidings. The 'Tutbury Jennie' local passenger service to Burton ceased in 1960 and Tutbury station was among those closed to passengers in November 1966. However, a new station, Tutbury & Hatton, opened in 1989 and is the last stop for most DMUs from Crewe to Derby, 11½ miles away. *LGRP*

Below: Class G 4-4-0 No 171 was one of four built by John H. Adams in 1910 for heavy express services, including Derby-Crewe, some of which were extended to Llandudno in summer. No 171 is pictured on a stoutly-fenced stretch of line near Derby. *LRGP*

Right: Tender piled high with coal, No 171 departs from Derby Midland station with a Crewe train in 1920. All four Class G locomotives survived until displaced by the LMS standardisation programme, being withdrawn 1929-33. No 171 was given two LMS numbers: 598 and finally 5413.
Hugh B. Oliver Collection

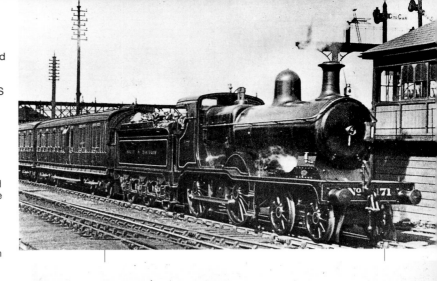

Centre right: The Crewe line (left) headed west from the Macclesfield line at Kidsgrove, called Harecastle for many years, six miles north of Stoke. Besides being a junction station, it was the terminus for trains which ran an infrequent service on the branch to Sandbach (Wheelock). *'Manifold' Collection*

Below: Kidsgrove, where NSR railway and canal meet. 'Crab' 2-6-0 No 42888 crosses the Trent & Mersey Canal just south of the station, before taking the Crewe line with a down freight. *M. Mensing*

N.S.R. RETURN HALF
Available for one journey
only on the day of issue
or the following day,
from Saturday to Monda
when issued on Saturda
Third Class
RUDYARD To
LEEK
D
Fare 3d.
TURN OVER   Rudy

Above: Alsager, two miles west of Harecastle, was served only by Crewe trains because the Sandbach and Audley lines left the main line a short distance to the east. Alsager was a typical NSR small town station, with goods yard and shed, small signalbox controlling a gated crossing, and a large station house with six tall chimney stacks. Platform canopies were supported by a row of cast-iron pillars. The scene is Edwardian. *R. W. Miller Collection*

Below: Crewe sees an NSR excursion returning from North Wales to the Potteries, headed by Class K 4-4-2T No 14. The train, of LNWR six-wheel compartment coaches, is passing under Spider Bridge between Crewe station and the works. The North Box in the fork of the West Coast and Chester line (left) dominated the junction until 1906. *IAL/Bucknall Collection*

Above: Most NSR services from Crewe ran all-stations to Derby, although not all called at Radway Green between Crewe and Alsager. An NSR 2-4-0 awaits departure from Crewe South bay. *LGRP*

Right: Crewe North Staffordshire Sidings box, awaiting demolition after closure in autumn 1983, when Crewe Signalling Centre opened. Three other NSR boxes dating from 1880 were also closed: Radway Green, Alsager Station and Alsager East. Level crossings at Radway Green and Alsager station are now controlled by closed circuit TV from the Crewe centre. *Author*

Below right: The south-facing spur linking the Kidsgrove line with Basford Hall marshalling yards was singled before closure in 1984. Two unidentified Class 25 diesel locomotives round the tight curve with check rail, before climbing to yard level. The West Coast main line over-bridge is left. *Author*

L.S.R. OUTWARD HALF
available for one journey
on day of issue only.
Second Class
ALSAGER To
LONGPORT
4243
Fare 1/1
1   TURN OVER

Above: Leek station, opened 1849, was an outstanding example of the civic consciousness and pride of the NSR founders, who gave the small town a station matching its importance. *Author's collection*

Below: Leek had an extensive goods yard adjacent to the station. Class 4F 0-6-0, BR No 44379, shunts a pick-up working. *P. G. Waterfield*

A Secondary Line and Branches

The Churnet Valley line of nearly 28 miles developed into a useful secondary through route between Manchester and Euston. It could always accommodate this traffic because there was only a limited passenger service through the valley.

NSR guide books stated that Churnet meant 'river of many windings' and that is how generations of enginemen regarded the section between Froghall and Uttoxeter, sharply curved because of being built on the course of the drained Caldon Canal. It was one of the earliest examples of such a scheme in Britain. An unusual problem which faced the railway builders was having to avoid interruption of traffic from Oakamoor Copper Works in the period between canal closure and railway completion.

The Churnet Valley line opened on 13 July 1849. Leek, the only intermediate town, was given a station with a colonnade, befitting its importance. Uttoxeter got three stations. All survived until the junction of the Churnet and Crewe-Derby lines was made triangular in 1881 and a new station built. It remains in use, although no longer as a junction.

Froghall, in one of the narrowest and steepest parts of the Churnet Valley, became an interchange with the Caldon Low tramways, with which the NSR could claim an ancestry dating back to the days of George III — further than most railway companies in Britain.

In 1776 the owners of the Trent & Mersey Canal obtained powers to build a railway or plateway to carry stone from limestone quarries on Caldon Low hill to a basin 649ft below. The tramway of some four miles opened in 1777, but its route had changed by the time it passed to the NSR through the latter's purchase of the canal in 1847. Two years later, the new owners built a fourth route with three inclines gauged to 3ft 6in. It remained in use until the 1920s, although it lost much of its traffic when the standard gauge branch to the quarries was completed from Leek Brook Junction in 1905.

A tramway of a rather different character also had connections with the Churnet Valley line, although for a much shorter time. Electrified to an overhead system of only 200V dc, it climbed from Leek Brook to Staffordshire Lunatic Asylum above the valley. It carried only goods and coal when it opened in about 1900, but passengers, who reached Leek Brook on NSR trains, were able to use it from 1905 until 1920. It closed in 1954.

Below: Classes of 2-6-4Ts were a familiar sight on Churnet Valley stopping trains for many years. Fowler No 42355 has just left North Rode (with tall up platform building in the background) on an afternoon service made up of compartment stock, bound for Uttoxeter. *Norman Jones*

Left: After the withdrawal of public passenger services in November 1960, a number of workmen's services continued. In summer 1962, 2-6-4T No 42454 prepares to leave with the 4.30pm Leek-Uttoxeter. The platform water column had an extending arm.
I. G. Holt

Below left: Uttoxeter Dove Bank station on the Churnet Valley line, looking towards Derby. With Churnet Valley Junction and Bridge Street station, it was replaced in 1881 when a spur was built between the Derby and Churnet lines and the present station opened. Class A 2-4-0T No 6 of 1878 has a five-link coupling hanging from the buffer beam.
LGRP

Above right: The overhead-electrified Cheddleton Asylum Railway carried supplies to the hospital, and also visitors, who changed at a station which the NSR built at Leek Brook. The electric locomotive and coach, both four-wheel, had few windows. They are seen at Cheddleton in 1901.
Hugh B. Oliver Collection

Centre right: An all-stations service runs through a wooded section of the Churnet Valley near Oakamoor about 1910. The rake of close-coupled coaches is headed by Class B 2-4-0T No 28, built at Stoke in 1882 and withdrawn 40 years later. *R. W. Miller Collection*

Right: Oakamoor in the late 1870s, before rebuilding. 0-6-0 No 68, built in 1875 (and rebuilt 1886), is shunting the station yard.
R. W. Miller Collection

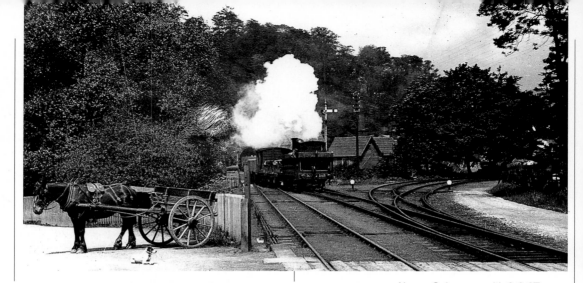

Above: Oakamoor with 0-6-0T No 145 shunting a short goods. The sidings right served Bolton's copper works. The horse, with cart, seems untroubled by the locomotive's presence. The ramp of down platform is in foreground.
R. W. Miller Collection

Left: A local service headed by Class B 2-4-0T No 27. Churnet Valley trains were often crowded on Wednesdays and Saturdays, which were market days in Leek. Cheap market tickets — third class only — could be used on most trains from the first services of the day: the 6.25am from Ashbourne to Macclesfield and the 7.10am from the Macclesfield.
R. W. Miller Collection

Right: A local train at Oakamoor, headed by Class A No 52. Built as a 2-4-0T at Stoke in 1879, it was rebuilt as a 2-4-2T in 1898 and was not withdrawn until 1932. A poster advertises an excursion to Rhyl. *Ian Allan Library*

Below: Cheddleton station, now the headquarters of the preserved Churnet Valley Railway, is attracting tourists to one of the prettiest parts of Staffordshire. Contemporary NSR guides stated that the Churnet line had been truly described as 'one of the most picturesque in the kingdom'. *J. A. Peden*

Right: Rudyard in the early 1880s. No 15 of Class 38 was built by Dubs in 1875. Like other stations on the line, it had up and down signals on the same post. *IAL/Bucknall Collection*

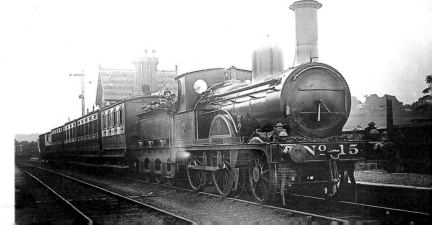

Sandbach branch

The 6½-mile Sandbach branch from the Harecastle-Crewe branch (as it was often called) at Lawton Junction, Alsager, was opened to the Wheelock district of Sandbach on 21 January 1852, but was not extended to the Crewe-Manchester main line at Wheelock Junction, at the south end of the LNWR station, until winter 1866.

The section, though busy with goods and mineral traffic, including that from several important salt works, never had a regular passenger service, although a service of three weekday passenger trains each way was introduced between Harecastle and Sandbach (Wheelock) in summer 1893. That was more than 40 years after it opened to goods — one of the longest periods recorded on the railways of Britain between the introduction of goods and passenger traffic on a branch.

Ashbourne branch

In 1852 Rocester, four miles north of Uttoxeter, became the junction of the 6¾-mile branch to the busy market town of Ashbourne, where London-Manchester stage coaches changed horses. That was three years after the Churnet line had been completed.

There was a three-year lag between authorisation and the start of construction because of opposition by the NSR shareholders. They claimed that Ashbourne was a somewhat remote town which could wait for a railway. Instead, they wanted the company to build lines to join those of other companies and provide far more lucrative two-way flows of traffic.

An unusual stipulation in the Act was that the railway was not to pass within 60yd of Ashbourne parish church. Noted for its spire of just over 200ft, NSR tourist guides were later to describe it as 'the pride of the Peak'.

In 1899 the branch became a through route when the LNWR opened its Buxton-Ashbourne line, incorporating parts of the Cromford & High Peak Railway and building a line south from Parsley Hay to Ashbourne.

'The new line not only renders accessible a district quite off the beaten track,' stated a contemporary guide book, 'but it gives the LNWR

Right: The first railway to reach Ashbourne was a branch of almost seven miles from the Churnet Valley at Rocester, four miles from Uttoxeter. Rocester had another classic NSR station with two tall and stout chimneys which passengers probably never noticed! *LGRP*

Below: Clifton, one of two intermediate branch stations, was renamed Clifton (Mayfield) in 1893. The scene depicted is in 1890, before a small signalbox was built to control the level crossing. The building in the background is prominently signed 'corn mill'. *Ian Allan Library*

Right: Ashbourne about 1880, with the goods yard and shed (right). 0-6-0 No 100 (Robert Stephenson & Co, 1860) heads a goods train and a Sharp 2-4-0T stands in front of the original NSR passenger station. *'Manifold' Collection*

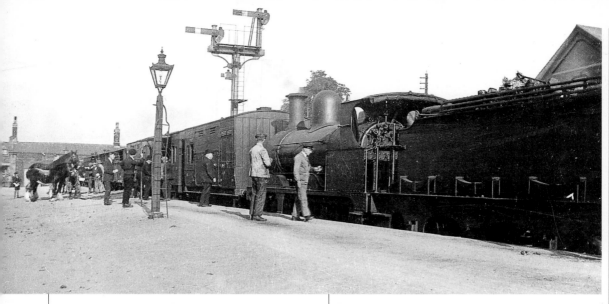

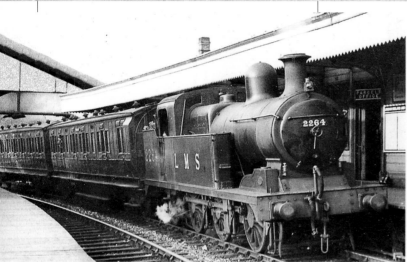

Above: Ashbourne on a horse and cattle fair day, when livestock special trains ran. The white-collared driver stands beside his unidentified 0-6-0.
'Manifold' Collection

Left: The scene at Ashbourne changed dramatically in 1899, when the LNWR linked it with Buxton and gave Ashbourne one of its standard design stations. The LNWR began local services between Buxton and Burton (Station Street) via Tutbury. The NSR presence at Buxton lingered long after Grouping. On 3 May 1934, H. C. Casserley found a train from Buxton headed by former NSR 'New L' 0-6-2T No 2264, Stoke-built in 1921. It was sold by the LMS in 1936.

a desirable alternative express route from Manchester to London via Buxton, Burton-on-Trent, Nuneaton and Rugby.' A joint station replaced that of the NSR which the people of Ashbourne had criticised for years, especially its lack of waiting accommodation.

The Midland Railway introduced a daily through coach service to St Pancras to try to attract tourists to 'the romantic scenery of Dovedale'. But later the area was better served by the LNWR.

Biddulph Valley branch

In 1854, two years after Ashbourne was added to the map of the infant NSR, came authorisation of the Potteries, Biddulph & Congleton Railway, completed under threats from mine owners already exploiting the coal-rich valley. They said that if the NSR did not build a line to serve it, they would build their own.

The Biddulph Valley line left the main line just south of Stoke station and ran 14 miles to Congleton, where it had its own terminus at Brunswick Wharf and a steeply-curved spur, climbing to the main line close to one of the two imposing viaducts.

The rural charm of the valley had been destroyed before the NSR arrived, for as the *Macclesfield Courier* noted on its opening in 1860: 'Within the last decade roaring furnaces have opened their ponderous jaws and are belching forth

Above: The Biddulph Valley branch pierced the heart of the industrial Potteries. The scene in 1912, is of the branch passing under the approach to the sidings of Chell Colliery, one of the biggest in the coalfield. Fencing of Chell Halt, opened in 1910, is bottom right. Empty wagons, including one of the Chatterley Whitfield fleet (left), are being pulled by *Alice*, a saddle tank built by the Yorkshire Engine Co in 1876. *'Manifold' Collection*

Right: Biddulph Valley passenger services were an early economy of the LMS, which withdrew them in November 1927, but the line remained busy for mineral traffic, not closing until open cast coal traffic from Ford Green ceased in March 1979. On 1 May 1967, dirty Class 8F 2-8-0 No 48151, hauling empty coal wagons, takes the Biddulph line at Milton Junction. The line to Leek Brook is left. *M. G. Fell*

Below right: Sand from Biddulph to Stoke passing Ford Green on 1 May 1967. The signalman has just collected the token and walked across the recently severed up line. *M. G. Fell*

volumes of smoke and liquid fire — the bowels of the earth are being dug out and converted to the requirements of the age'. From those 'bowels' in 1900, a million tons of coal was dug from the Chatterley Whitfield pit, making it the first in Britain to produce that amount in a year.

Like the Sandbach branch, this was a line on which a passenger service was a later addition, not being started until summer 1864. Biddulph Valley trains had to reverse over Congleton viaduct into the station, as the junction faced Macclesfield. Three weekday-only trains each way were shown in the same timetable as a rather more frequent Stoke-Leek service.

The PB&C Railway was among a number dating from the early 1850s which shaped the system in what a chairman later called 'a small octopus'.

In the 1860s, Stoke and Leek were joined by the Leek branch, which stemmed from the Biddulph branch at Milton Junction and joined the Churnet Valley, with which it was bracketed in company passenger timetables, at Leek Brook South Junction. It was authorised in 1863 but construction took four years because of difficulties in raising capital.

Burton upon Trent

Lack of money hampered construction of another branch, to Burton upon Trent, authorised at the same time as the Stoke-Leek branch. Nearly 3½ miles long, it gave the NSR access to the brewery town to compete against the well-entrenched Midland, LNWR and Great Northern. Not completed until 1 April 1868, just within the legal

Above: Long trains of empty four-wheel wagons tailed by brake vans were still a familiar sight in the Biddulph Valley towards the last days of steam. Stanier 2-8-0 No 48768 climbs from Ford Green to Whitfield Colliery on 1 May 1967. *M. G. Fell*

Left: Milton, five miles from Stoke, was among several wayside stations closed when Stoke-Leek passenger services fell victim to road competition in May 1956. For years several trains connected with a local service between Leek and Rushton and formed part of the same timetable. *LGRP*

Right: Double-framed 0-6-0 No 87 as rebuilt in 1890, is about to leave Burton with the regular Wellingborough goods. The tender is piled high with hand-stacked coal to avoid having to replenish supplies at the Midland shed at Wellingborough. *IAL/Bucknall Collection*

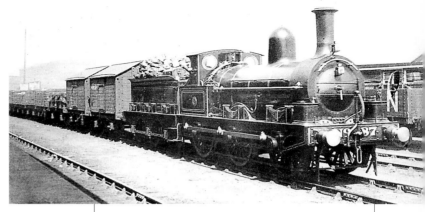

Below: Burton upon Trent retained a passenger service over ex-NSR metals to Tutbury — the 'Tutbury Jennie' — until summer 1960, although the three intermediate stations, including Horninglow, closed more than a decade earlier on New Year's Day 1949. *LGRP*

Right: The 'Tutbury Jennie' at Tutbury, in charge of Class B 2-4-0T No 2, built at Stoke in 1890. *IAL/Bucknall Collection*

time limit, it ran from Marston Junction to the Midland, three-quarters of a mile north of Burton station. A mile-long branch gave the NSR access to running powers into the LNWR goods station at Horninglow Street.

From Burton, apart from beer, the NSR carried timber, plaster slabs, engineering and chemical products. It marshalled traffic at Stretton Junction, Horninglow Bridge sidings and station yards.

Longton, Adderley Green & Bucknall Railway

The Chatterley Whitfield Company owned five lucrative coal mines along the route of what became the Longton, Adderley Green & Bucknall Railway, always a mineral line. It was developed and owned by a company formed with the approval of NSR shareholders. The line, of less than four miles, ran from the Biddulph Valley branch at Botteslow Junction to the Derby line at Millfield Junction, near Normacot.

It opened in 1875 and, after taking it over 20 years later, the NSR cut the line in two so that it could get higher revenues from having to haul coal from local pits greater distances over its own system.

Branches north and west of Stoke

One branch, included in the NSR's 1847 Act of Incorporation, was a half-mile connection from

Continued on page 44.

Above: A frequent passenger service was maintained for years, between Stoke and Newcastle-under-Lyme, over the eastern two miles of the Market Drayton branch. Class D 0-6-0T No 152 of 1898 is seen with a Stoke-bound train at Newcastle. Behind is a short bay and a single track into the town goods yard, built on a canal bed. *'Manifold' Collection*

Below: At Newcastle, the fireman of '8F' 2-8-0 No 48110 prepares to catch the token from the station signalman for possession through the single bore Newcastle tunnel. The mineral train is bound for Stoke on 23 January 1965. *M. G. Fell*

Right: Class 8F 2-8-0 No 48600 passes Ketley's Sidings, heading towards Silverdale with a coal train. The sidings were the junction of the short Pool Dam branch (right). *M. G. Fell*

Centre right: A sign at the west end of Silverdale Tunnel warned staff that both tracks were single tracks (of the Market Drayton and Audley lines) on which trains ran in both directions. Pictured 10 May 1964. *M. G. Fell*

Below: Keele, 5¼ miles from Stoke, lost its passenger services through two economies: the LMS withdrew services to Alsager Road over the Audley line in 1931 and Stoke-Market Drayton trains ceased in May 1956. The view is westward: the Market Drayton line is left; Audley, right. The scene is eight years after Keele closed to passengers. *M. G. Fell*

Above: The Madeley Chord, connecting the Market Drayton branch with the West Coast main line, nine miles south of Crewe, was laid on the trackbed of a spur built by the NSR but never completed. The bridge carrying the branch spans the main line in the background. *R. W. Miller*

Left: Madeley Road, within sight of the West Coast main line to the east, was so remote that it was closed by the LMS in 1931. This is a 1952 scene, looking towards Stoke. *LGRP*

Below left: Class A 2-4-0T No 35 at Pipe Gate, 'for Woore' as it was shown in timetables, c1895. Three years later No 35 was rebuilt as a 2-4-2T. *LGRP*

Above right: Pipe Gate signalbox was prominently positioned on the up platform, while the station building, with overhanging roof rather than platform canopy, was at rail level. *LGRP*

Right: Norton in Hales, another remote station in the Shropshire countryside, was three miles east of Market Drayton. *LGRP*

Left: Audley was served by trains between Stoke and Harecastle (Kidsgrove) via Keele. Railmotors were used on some part-way services in Edwardian days. Diglake Colliery (right) was connected to the branch. *J. A. Peden*

Below left: The 1½-mile Apedale branch, which stemmed from the Market Drayton line, served the extensive complex of the Midland Coal & Iron Co. It ran its own mineral and workmen's trains over the NSR. Those between Apedale and the Pool Dam branch had to reverse at Apedale Junction. *A. C. Baker*

Bottom left: The Apedale branch gave access to a mineral line to the large Holditch Colliery. In summer 1964, 'Black Five' No 45037 with a loaded coal train joins the branch from the colliery line. The locomotive has the allocation of 'Stoke' lettered on the front buffer beam. *M. G. Fell*

Right: Silverdale's small station building is dominated by a Holditch Colliery loading bunker. Class 20 diesels Nos 20113 and 20055 arrive with empty wagons, while HAAs are being loaded for a service to Ironbridge Power Station. The date is April 1988, when the main flow from Holditch was to Llanwern. *Paul Shannon*

the main line at Newcastle Junction to Knutton Junction with the Pool Dam line. Later it was a strategic springboard from which the NSR was extended west from the Potteries to the country areas of the Shropshire border. A line was built not so much to serve those sparsely populated areas, but to keep out of the Potteries several other companies, including the LNWR and GWR. Other predators were the promoters of a number of companies which failed to get authorisation.

Little was done quickly. Money was tight and it seems likely that the NSR directors were hopeful that the big companies would lose interest in trying to invade the Potteries, accepting that it was perhaps more profitable simply to exchange traffic.

The scheme which finally took the NSR west to Market Drayton, 17 miles from Stoke, was authorised by one of two Acts of summer 1864. (The other was for a line from Silverdale via Audley, centre of extensive coal and ore deposits, to Alsager.) A spur was agreed between the Market Drayton line and the LNWR West Coast route at Madeley, but this was not built until the BR era.

At Market Drayton, the NSR joined the GWR, which had opened from Nantwich in 1864 and was to extend this secondary route to Wellington in 1867. It was part of a GWR attempt to establish an independent route between the West Midlands and Manchester, serving the Potteries with a branch from Madeley to Newcastle-under-Lyme. That was defeated by the combined opposition of the NSR and LNWR, as was a section planned by Paddington between Nantwich and Northwich.

But any hopes that the NSR had of being able to stay out of Shropshire were dashed when the Board of Trade, while allowing extra time for the construction of several authorised branches,

refused to include the Audley and Market Drayton lines. They were quickly built to comply with their Acts, although the company had to meet what were described as excessive compensation claims by landowners — a common feature during the era of Victorian railway building.

When the line opened in 1870, Market Drayton station was enlarged and put under the control of a joint stationmaster. The NSR staff consisted of three clerks and shunters, six signalmen, a ticket collector and four parcel porters. Additionally, the GWR had a staff of five goods clerks, a goods guard, one goods and two yard foremen, four goods porters, one checker and a lad porter. The NSR contributed towards the cost of Silverdale Junction signalbox.

A clue to how little the Stoke line was used was revealed by the magazine *Railway World* in September 1984, when it featured the line in LMS days. 'We have been unable to locate a picture of a train at Norton in Hales,' it admitted. Few enthusiasts travelled into the lonely rolling countryside of North Shropshire.

The Audley branch also opened in 1870, but only to mineral traffic. The line did not see a passenger service for another nine years. The service was sparse: five trains each way on weekdays, fewer on Saturdays and Sundays.

The Audley Act included branches to large pits at Jamage and Bignall Hill, also served by the Talk O'Th'Hill branch, which climbed the Harecastle ridge from the NSR main line at Chatterley Sidings. It had the steepest gradient on an NSR goods or mineral line of 1 in 36, falling for half a mile from Red Street towards Chatterley.

Chatterley Sidings were also the starting point of the 1½-mile Chesterton branch, which ran parallel with the Talk branch, to which it was joined until 1877 when the Talk branch became

too congested to handle traffic from a second branch.

The NSR system at the heart of the industrial Potteries was a web of short branches. Only four days before the Market Drayton Acts, the company obtained authority for two other lines: from Longport to Pinnox, called the Tunstall Lower branch, which formed a second link between the main line and the Biddulph Valley branch, and from Pinnox to Newfields, called the Tunstall Upper branch. Although not more than three-quarters of a mile long, there were hopes the Newfields branch might be extended over Harecastle ridge to Alsager and Crewe; NSR promoters were nothing if not visionary; but the hope was hardly strong, for branch construction took four years.

The Potteries Loop

Just one of the NSR's routes achieved immortal fame: the Loop line, beloved of the novelist Arnold Bennett. It was developed with nothing like the haste often associated with various lines of the period, for authorisation and construction of the seven-mile Loop, effectively a Potteries inner circle line, took twice that number of years.

It grew from a 1¼-mile branch, originally authorised in 1847, linking the growing town of Hanley to the main line at Etruria. It opened in 1861, but only for goods and mineral traffic; a passenger service did not follow until summer 1864. Not everyone was pleased. Because of the noise of trains and local furnaces, the North Staffordshire Infirmary moved from Hanley, where it had been built in the year of the Battle of Waterloo.

It is now nearly 30 years since I learned of the immediate success of the opening of the Hanley

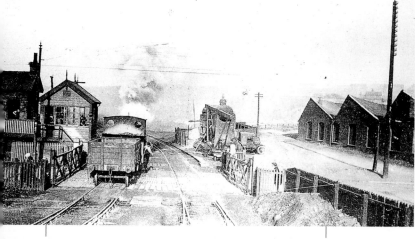

Above: The Pinnox branch, a short, busy link between the main line at Longport and the Loop line, was also linked to industrial lines. A loaded coal train prepares to leave the Whitfield-Pinnox Mineral Railway at Pinnox Junction. Class D 0-6-0T No 139 was built at Stoke in 1893 — a few years before it was photographed.
R. W. Miller Collection

Left: A view from the Loop line of Pinnox Crossing and Box, with Whitfield locomotive *Edward VII* shunting by the Pinnox Paddy platform (right). *Dr J. R. Hollick*

Below left: The heart of the Potteries was ensnared by a web of lines connected to the NSR. This is a mid-1950s scene from Pinnox viaduct on the Loop line, with the Whitfield-Pinnox Mineral Railway curving west towards Pinnox Junction. The line in the centre leads to Brownhills Wharf. The town is Tunstall. *Dr J. R. Hollick*

Right: The southern junction of the Loop line was at Etruria Junction. The scene is in winter 1952, before 25kV electrification of the main line, heading north towards Kidsgrove (left). The Loop curved sharply and climbed away into the Shelton Iron and Steel Works (right). Grange and Etruria yards are centre.
F. W. Shuttleworth

branch to passengers, by researching the NSR Board minutes then stored in the BRB Records Office at Old Oak — a building in which the aroma of GWR steam encouraged flagging researchers! Laboriously, in an era in which tape recorders were banned, I wrote in Gregg shorthand the details of how local people pressed the NSR directors to extend the Loop north to Burslem and Tunstall. The outcome was an Act of 1865 for a line from Hanley back to the main line at Kidsgrove.

But a general trade depression, rooted in the American Civil War, set-in the following year and became so serious that the Board sought legal powers under the Abandonment of Railways Act 1850. Shareholders readily agreed, but local authorities were angered. Burslem Board of Health held a special meeting and decided to offer 'the utmost opposition against the iniquitous attempt to deprive the district of the railway accommodation so long needed, and for want of which its interests have been so largely sacrificed'. The situation was resolved when a House of Commons Committee ignored the shareholders and rejected the application to abandon the rest of the branch.

Faced with a shortage of money, the directors examined the possibility of completing the Loop as a narrow gauge light railway, as gradients would be steep and the distance short. They considered using narrow gauge Fairlie double-ended locomotives like those on the Festiniog Railway, but problems that a change of gauge might cause led to construction being resumed to standard gauge.

Work soon began on the summit level between Pitts Hill and Newchapel, with a locomotive put on rails at Turnhurst Hall, the home of the canal engineer James Brindley who had died there in 1772.

When the Loop reached Burslem in November 1873 a new station was opened at Hanley. On completion of an extension to Tunstall a month later, a local paper noted that spectators seemed to show as much interest in trains as dog racing and rabbit coursing in a nearby field.

The Loop was completed to Kidsgrove in November 1875 by a section which, north of Goldenhill, was only single track. It was so steeply graded — 1 in 40 — that only down trains called at Kidsgrove Halt.

About this time, an LNWR guide reflected on the rapid growth of the Potteries, noting that the district, which a century earlier had been a bleak and rugged landscape, very sparse of inhabitants, 'now teems with active life, and occupies an honourable place among the world's great workshops'.

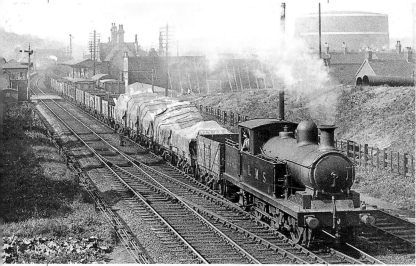

Above: Cobridge looking north, 1952. A Stoke-bound train approaches the well-kept station with newly-painted wooden buildings, gas lamps and tidy gardens. *LGRP*

Left: The NSR scene changed little after Grouping, as exemplified in this study of a 'New L' 0-6-2T of 1908, renumbered LMS 2246, passing Tunstall station with a long goods working. *F. R. Hebron*

Below left: The Newfields branch ran about half a mile from the Loop line at Tunstall to a small goods yard. It was one of three branches which the Light Railway Commissioners refused to allow the NSR to operate as a Light Railway. In summer 1953, ex-LNWR 'Cauliflower' 0-6-0 No 58382 shunts the yard. *F. W. Shuttleworth*

Above right: Newchapel & Goldenhill station looking south towards Stoke. A 35mph speed restriction sign is on the down line by the sleeper-crossing. The northern 1¾miles of the Loop from here to Kidsgrove (Liverpool Road) were single. *Prof C. L. Mowat*

Lower right: Class B 2-4-0T No 25, built at Stoke 1882, is about to run round a Loop line train at Normacot — hence no lamp. The guard, smartly uniformed with gold braid hat, poses with driver and fireman. *R. W. Miller Collection*

Loop line trains made up of rakes of short four-wheel coaches pulled by small tank locomotives conquered sharp gradients and tight curves and ran through a landscape of steelworks, collieries, coking plants and brickworks.

A long-projected scheme which never came to fruition, but might have altered the railway map of the inner Potteries had it done so, was for a passenger branch between the Biddulph Valley and Loop lines. Dr Hollick felt it would have been 'a valuable northward extension of the Loop'. Eventually it was built as a private mineral line by the Chatterley Whitfield Company.

The Loop was always at the core of the NSR. Its passenger services were not confined to its 7¼ miles. Some continued north from Kidsgrove to Congleton and south of Stoke to Uttoxeter.

The Loop was connected to a number of short but busy mineral branches of the type for which the NSR became renowned. The most important of them — the Pinnox, Grange and Newfields — were included in an exhaustive illustrated history, *The Potteries Loop Line* by Allan C. Baker.

Macclesfield, Bollington & Marple Railway

The NSR created a route into Manchester, and also Yorkshire, independent of the LNWR, by opening a joint line with the Manchester, Sheffield & Lincolnshire (later Great Central Railway), which was extending its network in South Manchester in the 1860s.

There was no fight between companies: Euston being prepared to let the MB&M bill pass through Parliament provided the MS&L withdrew support for two independent railways in south Cheshire which were to create a 26-mile line from

the NSR at Macclesfield to Warrington. It was never built.

The Macclesfield, Bollington & Marple Railway was incorporated in 1864 to construct an 11-mile line from a junction with the NSR between Macclesfield Central and Hibel Road stations to the MS&L at Marple.

A lack of finance caused by a general trade depression delayed construction. Passenger services began in August 1869 and goods in March 1871. The single line, soon doubled, was worked by the MS&L and later the Great Central.

It was taken over as a joint company by the MS&L and NSR in 1871 and was known as The Macclesfield Committee. In 1908 it changed its name to the GC/NSR Joint and in that form it passed into history as the last surviving part of the

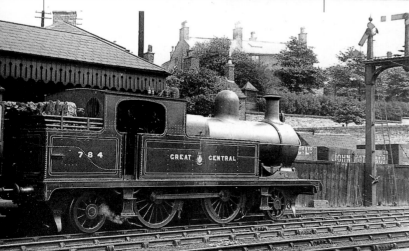

Above: Middlewood was a rather remote wooden station on the Macclesfield, Bollington & Marple. Former Great Central 4-4-2T BR No 67422 is on a Manchester (London Road)-Macclesfield Central stopping service in August 1950. The station lost its NSR nameboard when it was renamed Middlewood Higher the following year. *N. Fields*

Centre left: A former GCR 0-6-2T, BR No 69347, pauses at Middlewood, also in August 1950. An LMS & LNER signpost on the A6, the main road through the area, warned that both Middlewood stations — that of the LMS was on the Stockport-Buxton branch — were a 10min walk away. *N. Fields*

Below left: Class F2 2-4-2Ts were among locomotives used by the GCR when the line was GC/NSR Joint. No 784 is seen at Macclesfield. *N. Fields*

NSR, because the title was not changed until Nationalisation.

In 1885, a spur was built at Middlewood between the MB&M and the LNWR Stockport-Buxton branch. Like the MB&M, the spur, which was entirely LNWR-owned, was never developed as a through route for passengers, services always being local between Macclesfield Central and Manchester London Road.

By the time a new joint station opened at Macclesfield in 1873, improved relations between the NSR and LNWR reduced what strategic value the MB&M enjoyed, because the NSR used the LNWR route via Stockport to reach Manchester, which was five miles shorter.

The NSR profile was never high on the MB&M because it was responsible for maintenance and engineering works, rather than staff and train operation, although the NSR introduced a limited summer service between Macclesfield and Buxton after the Middlewood spur opened.

The NSR in Cheshire

The MB&M was the most northerly of lines with which the NSR spilled over into counties bordering its own. As the company passes deeper into history, the extent and importance of its impact on the railways of Cheshire are often forgotten.

It owned the Harecastle-Congleton-Macclesfield and Harecastle-Crewe sections of the main lines; the spur at Crewe to Basford Hall marshalling yard, sidings at the approach to Crewe and a coal yard on the West Coast main line north of the station (reached using running powers). Although the yard closed some years ago, Coal Yard box, which controlled entry, is still operational as a fringe box to Crewe Signalling Centre.

The Sandbach branch was wholly in Cheshire, together with the first mile of the Harecastle (Alsager Junction)-Keele branch, the northern three miles of the Churnet Valley line from North Rode, the 1½-mile tip of the Biddulph Valley branch between Congleton Lower Junction and Brunswick Wharf, and the spur to Congleton Upper Junction.

In summer, NSR Llandudno expresses could be seen passing through country stations between Crewe and Chester as they ran across the Cheshire Plain between Harecastle and the Welsh border.

Below: An infrequent passenger service on the four-mile Cheadle branch from the Derby main line at Cresswell was incorporated into Loop line timetables. Here, a Loop line train prepares to leave the original station with its small buildings and an unsurfaced platform. Locomotive No 12 has been rebuilt at Stoke as a 2-4-2T. *H. B. Oliver Collection*

Above: A charming spring 1962 study of Cheadle terminus, showing the neat station as rebuilt in 1910, goods shed and yard. BR-liveried 2-6-4T No 42665 is shunting empty mineral wagons. *Leslie Sandler*

Last branches

The Knotty was tied into final shape by several short branches, each highly individual, built towards the close of the Victorian era and through the Edwardian years. They ran to Cheadle, Trentham, Caldon Low quarries and the village of Waterhouses, which became the terminus of the narrow gauge Leek & Manifold Valley Light Railway. Additionally, in 1899, the NSR acquired another connection with the LNWR when the Ashbourne branch became a through route to Buxton from the south.

The Cheadle Railway

The market town of Cheadle, hub of a small yet busy coalfield, was among the first which the NSR selected to have a railway, being included in the company's original prospectus of 1845. But it was also the last town of any size in NSR territory to get one because, after early hopes of being rail connected were dashed, it had to wait until the Cheadle Railway Mineral & Land Company Ltd got an Act in 1888. The NSR got powers to subscribe £10,000, but six years elapsed before its shareholders approved.

Construction of a four-mile branch from the Derby line at Cresswell occupied almost a decade. The first 1¼ miles to the village of Totmonslow, later renamed Tean, were opened in 1892 by the Cheadle Railway.

The rest of the branch was among the last stretches of railway completed in the reign of Queen Victoria, who died in January 1901, only three weeks later. Its passenger service was incorporated in that of the Loop line. The NSR took over the local company in 1907.

Leek & Manifold Valley Light Railway

One of the lesser reasons for construction of the eight-mile, narrow gauge Leek & Manifold Valley Light Railway through lonely valleys was the concern of traders at Leek that the LNWR Ashbourne-Buxton line would make it easier for people to get to markets in those towns rather than Leek.

Right: The Leek & Manifold Valley Light Railway (1904-34) was one of four British 2ft 6in gauge lines, another being the Welshpool & Llanfair. An L&M train with first and third class carriages, is seen in about 1908, headed by one of the line's two 2-6-4Ts, No 2 *J. B. Earle.* *R. W. Miller Collection*

Centre right: Opening day, 27 June 1904, when some official guests used bogie wagons built for milk churn traffic because two of the four passenger coaches had not been delivered on time. *Ian Allan Library*

Below: The delightful scenery failed to attract large crowds. Ladies in long white dresses and men wearing blazers and white flannels were not dressed to stray from the platform at Thor's Cave, one of the numerous halts in the eight miles between Hulme End and Waterhouses. The locomotive 'fleet' is running back to back. *LGRP*

The Duke of Devonshire cut the first sod of the light railway in October 1899. It was authorised from Waterhouses, a moorland village almost 10 rail miles from Leek, to Hulme End, less than two miles from Hartington on the new LNWR line.

The L&MVLR, opened in 1904, was one of only four built to the 2ft 6in gauge in Britain: the most famous of the others was the Welshpool & Llanfair. The Leek & Manifold was far from being an NSR enterprise, for part of its construction costs were borne by Staffordshire County Council and the Government. For its part, the NSR had to build two standard gauge feeder lines. They were authorised under the same Light Railway Order of March 1899. The first was a 4½-mile link from the Churnet Valley at Cheddleton (later Leek Brook) Junction to Ipstones, which gave the NSR a new summit of 1,000ft above sea level near

Ipstones. The other was an extension to Waterhouses of almost equal length and giving access to Caldon Low quarries, perpetually leased to the NSR, which produced more than 500,000 tons of limestone a year.

Branch construction caused fresh controversy at Leek because traders feared they would suffer through Waterhouses getting a direct rail link with Stoke. They knew that W. D. Phillipps, who had then been General Manager of the NSR for more than 20 years, hated Leek and everything about it so far as the company was concerned. To pacify critics, the NSR had to build a spur at Leek Brook Junction to allow a direct service between Leek and Waterhouses. It was shown in Bradshaw's timetables as three weekday trains and a single one on Sundays, augmented on Wednesdays and Saturdays.

Left: Hulme End. The large nameboard proclaiming 'Hulme End for Hartington' is beside the passenger coach. Hartington was two miles away on the LNWR Buxton-Ashbourne branch. The locomotive shed was dominated by a high water tower. There is a substantial coal stack (right). *LGRP*

Below left: The L&MV was worked by the NSR but owned by a separate company. It was a financial disaster despite many innovations, including the use of transporter wagons. An NSR six-wheel milk van stands on a transporter beside a loading platform at Ecton. The passenger coach is on the main line. *LGRP*

Above right: Shunting at Waterhouses in the early 1930s. The wagon is on a short transporter. The hinged rail of the transporter is lying flat. *LGRP*

Centre right: The line was a copy of the Barsi Light Railway, a 79-mile line in India which had locomotives and rolling stock built to 'Calthrop's Patent'. In contrast to the L&M it was financially successful, paying dividends of around 2%. Locomotive No 1 *E. R. Calthrop* stands beside the coal stack at Hulme End in 1931. *LGRP*

Bottom right: Waterhouses pictured soon after opening. One contemporary tourist guide described the country it traversed as one of many 'ups and downs necessitating sharp curves and severe gradients'. *LGRP*

Above: Bradnop (seen here) and Ipstones were the only two stations in the 10 miles between Leek and Waterhouses via a north-to-east curve from the Churnet Valley line at Leek Brook junction. Shortly before the Waterhouses branch opened in summer 1905, a Class D 0-6-0T pulls a saloon with a balcony at the far end. Ground frame on platform (left). The second track is still to be laid. *LGRP*

Below: An early scene at Waterhouses, again with tank engine and saloon. The value to the NSR of the line from Leek Brook was not so much the connection at Waterhouses with the L&M, but in providing a standard gauge outlet for stone traffic from Caldon Low Quarries, ending transhipment from the narrow gauge incline to the Churnet Valley at Froghall.
H. B. Oliver Collection

Above: Bradnop remained open to goods until May 1964. Three months later, Class 5 4-6-0 No 44844 passes the small, derelict goods shed, with a limestone working from Caldon Low. *J. A. Powell*

Right: There was an eight-year gap between the withdrawal of the Leek-Waterhouses passenger service by the LMS in autumn 1935 and complete closure of the final mile of the Waterhouses branch from Caldon Junction, a wartime economy of winter 1943. An LMS milk train is seen at Waterhouses, headed by NSR 'New C' class 0-6-4T No 70, renumbered LMS No 2043 before withdrawal in 1935, when only 21 years old. *LGRP*

Trentham Park branch

The Trentham Park branch, running only 1¼ miles from the main line at Trentham, one of the original stations on the first section of NSR main line between Stoke and Norton Bridge, was, in 1907, the last of the company's lines to be authorised. It opened three years later, when railmotors were being used to meet road competition.

The branch served Trentham Hall, which became pleasure gardens to which local people flocked, after being abandoned by the Duke of Sutherland because of smells from the River Trent.

World War 1 delayed plans for the Trentham, Newcastle-under-Lyme & Silverdale Light Railway, by which the branch was to be extended four miles to the Pool Dam line, to form a western circular railway through growing residential areas. The extension was never built and for years its memorial was a large girder bridge across London Road at Trentham, demolished for scrap during World War 2.

The fortunes of the Trentham Park branch varied through the years. The first setback occurred when the intermediate station at Hanford Road closed only three years after opening.

Stafford & Uttoxeter Railway

The NSR's allusion to its milk vans being seen on passenger trains of the Great Northern and other companies may have arisen from its associations with the Stafford & Uttoxeter Railway. This small company was incorporated in summer 1862 to build a 13-mile line from the NSR at Bromshall Junction, two miles from Uttoxeter, to Stafford, with running powers over the NSR into Uttoxeter. A connection, never built, was authorised at Weston, between Stone and Colwich. The independent company was in financial difficulties from the start. Construction of the S&UR took five years and it existed only until 1881, when it was taken over by the GNR as part of an ill-fated attempt to reach North Wales. Stafford, which became the most westerly place on the GNR, was never regarded as a terminal.

One of the S&UR's claims to inclusion in the history of the NSR was that its service, headed 'Derby, Burton and Ashbourne, with Stafford G.N.', occupied the title page in NSR passenger timetables for some years. The reason remains obscure; the likelihood is that the table, showing six weekday trains and one Sunday train each way, conveniently fitted space available below the names and addresses of NSR directors and the names of senior officers.

Left: The Stafford & Uttoxeter had pride of place in NSR timetables with a service, generally of six daily trains, between Nottingham Great Northern and Stafford. In GNR tables the S&U was linked into Grantham, Nottingham, Derby, Burton and Uttoxeter tables. Stafford Common station, 1¾ miles away, was reached 5min after departure from Stafford LNWR. The dilapidated Stafford Common station is seen in 1957 — 18 years after it lost its regular passenger services. *Geoffrey Bannister*

Years of Growth

'In trying to force the smaller line to its will the LNWR gave one of the best examples of double dealing that has been recorded in the not over-savoury history of the "Premier Line".'

That was the verdict of the 'Manifold' group in their history of the NSR, of the outcome of early battles between the companies which continued for years. There were frequent rumours of impending take-over by Euston, but all proved false as the sturdy and profitable NSR asserted its independence. It continually complained that Euston was not giving it the volume of traffic to which it was entitled after legal rulings.

Euston's attempts at domination forced the NSR to negotiate an agreement in 1849. While it gave the NSR 'every reasonable facility' over LNWR lines and a share of through traffic, it also allowed the LNWR to use the Potteries line for direct Manchester traffic. Legal battles quickly followed.

The NSR planned to retaliate by developing fresh ties with other neighbours, gaining access, for instance, to Manchester and West Yorkshire via Marple by building the Macclesfield, Bollington & Marple Railway with the Manchester, Sheffield & Lincolnshire. Less successful was an attempt to establish an independent route between the Potteries and London, using the Midland Railway branch from Leicester to the Great Northern at Hitchin, the Midland main line to St Pancras not yet having been built.

This was at a time when the NSR was being attacked from within by a group of militant shareholders who forced an internal probe into the company's affairs. Directors were cleared of making wrong decisions, but they claimed the investigation

Below: Weight restrictions on the NSR section barred several classes of large express locomotives from handling Euston-Manchester services but ex-LNWR 'Claughton' 4-6-0s were allowed. In LMS days, No 5920 *George Macpherson* heads a down express through Trentham where ex-NSR cattle trucks are stabled in sidings. *Real Photographs*

Above: Two years after Grouping, an ex-NSR 'New M' class 0-4-4T heads a local train on the West Coast main line near Stafford. The locomotive, then only five years old, was not scrapped until 1939. *LGRP*

Left: The importance of the Potteries route to the LNWR was evident in the 1870s, when Euston partly met the cost of improving the Stone-Colwich section. Weston & Ingestre was among the neatly designed NSR country stations. In 1951, the station remained intact, although four years had passed since the withdrawal of a sparse stopping service. *LGRP*

Below left: Consall Bridge over the Churnet was among substantial structures which replaced original timber bridges in the 1880s. The locomotive is Sharp Stewart 2-4-0T No 41 of 1875, rebuilt as a 2-4-2T in 1899. The passenger coach probably dated from the 1850s. *LGRP*

Right: Clean and shiny Class C 0-6-4T No 30 is pictured with a goods train near Derby, 1923. The first wagon is one of the South Eastern & Chatham fleet. *LGRP*

Below: The typical NSR goods train may have been short compared with those of bigger companies, but it was full of variety, often being made up of wagons of different shapes and sizes. Here, Class E Beyer Peacock 0-6-0 of 1874 No 119 with well-filled tender is in charge. *IAL/Bucknall Collection*

had placed them in a weak position while negotiating a new agreement with the LNWR. It took effect in spring 1850, but led to fresh dissent with the LNWR and the Midland Railway.

Relations with Euston finally improved from 1866 when Euston was given running powers over the entire NSR, which, in return, got similar facilities over present — and future — routes to Wolverhampton, Birmingham, Manchester and Liverpool.

NSR trains could now reach Birmingham via Norton Bridge, and Liverpool via Crewe and Warrington, and also over Runcorn Bridge across the Mersey, completed in 1869. Running powers totalled 160 miles, roughly equal to the mileage which the NSR had either built or been authorised to construct.

Euston got powers to operate two fast passenger and two goods trains each way between London and Manchester via Colwich or Norton Bridge — except on Good Friday and Christmas Day. The LNWR regarded the agreement as excellent, not least because if relations between the companies became hostile, or the NSR was taken over, it would retain the right of access to the Potteries.

And there was a flurry of take-over activity a few years later. It began when the NSR directors decided to sell or lease the company to some of its larger neighbours. The LNWR, Midland, Great Northern and Manchester, Sheffield & Lincolnshire discussed the possibility of guaranteeing the NSR 4% a year.

No attempt was made to contact the NSR and the suggestion was quietly dropped as the big companies failed to agree among themselves as to how much each would get from a deal.

The next move was made in 1875 by the MS&L, with an amalgamation scheme which both boards and NSR shareholders approved. A stumbling block though, was found to be the inability of the NSR to make big concessions over traffic arrangements because of ties with the LNWR, while the MS&L was handicapped by its links with the GNR. Talks were ended when the NSR directors realised the MS&L finances were no stronger than their own.

Take-over continued to be advocated by some shareholders wanting better returns on their investments. In 1877 one of them suggested the lease of the NSR to the Midland, since it was unlikely that the GNR or MS&L would give a better price, while the LNWR, he contended, wanted the company for 'an old song'.

When the issue was discussed a year later, the Chairman said it must be remembered that the NSR had a small mileage and had to collect traffic for the large companies which surrounded it. They made profits from good mileages while the NSR had to do a great deal of hard work for comparatively little return. The NSR could never be as good a paying line.

In the mid-1870s, the NSR was paying dividends of just under 2% — about a third of those received by LNWR shareholders — but it was a healthy little company, carrying about 2¾ million passengers a year. Train operating costs were considered favourable with those of most companies, although it complained that Parliamentary freight rates did not take account of goods trains it had to run which called at 'everybody's siding' to pick up or leave a wagon.

Euston's influence became clear in 1876 when it decided that the Stone-Colwich line should be relaid, partly at its own expense. Major improvement was necessary because the line had been little used for years, when through expresses had been routed via Norton Bridge to serve Stafford and there was scant local passenger or pick-up goods traffic.

NSR traffic increased towards the end of the century — as did expenses, as it became necessary to lay heavier track and replace more than 60 original timber and cast-iron viaducts and bridges with stronger ones of wrought-iron and stone, partly to carry heavier trains.

Because it had so many short mineral lines, NSR revenue fell during periods of economic depression. In 1885, for example, there was concern about a drop in the volume of bitter beer sent from Burton. The company was suffering financially from light loads and short trains, which cost almost as much to operate as those more heavily loaded. In 1900-1, it was one of only four of Britain's 18 major companies that failed to increase goods mileage earnings.

In late Victorian times the NSR was reduced from being a 'nine penny line' to a 'six penny line' — tags relating to the short distances passengers travelled at low fares. The trend continued for years, the Chairman once complaining, 'We literally pile up passenger traffic by six pences.' He cited an unnamed station where in three Edwardian years, revenue was £2,625. Yet nearly 200,000 passengers had been booked.

A decade earlier, in the first half of 1891, first class passengers represented only 7½% of the total of 3¼ million carried. Efforts to encourage

Far left: Industry in the Churnet Valley increased during World War 1 and extra trains running before winter dawn were introduced. Workmen's weekly tickets advertised in November 1915 were issued subject to a number of conditions, one being that 'they must be produced each morning and night to be nipped'. *Author*

Right: In late Edwardian days, when people began travelling more for pleasure, the NSR tried to exploit the beauty of country areas close to the Potteries by issuing tourist and excursion tickets to 'places of great interest'. Because of competition from other companies, the public were 'particularly requested to ask for Tickets by the "North Stafford" Route and to see that such Tickets are supplied to them'. *Author*

Below: Three Beyer Peacock railmotors were introduced in 1905 to fight tram competition in areas around Stoke. They could seat nearly 50 third class passengers. Driving wheels were 3ft 8in. *R. Rushton*

NORTH STAFFORDSHIRE RAILWAY.

THE

"North Stafford" Route

IS THE

SHORTEST, QUICKEST, and BEST for both

GOODS AND PASSENGERS

BETWEEN

Leicester, Newark, Nottingham, Lincoln, Grantham, Boston, Cambridge, Bedford, Northampton, Market Harborough, Sheffield, Chesterfield, Derby, and Burton,

AND

Chester, Birkenhead, Liverpool, North, South, and Mid Wales, Ireland, Isle of Man, Buxton, Lancashire, and the North.

TOURIST TICKETS by this Route are issued from the former to the latter districts each Season ; also EXCURSION TICKETS (Day and Week-end) in most instances between the same points and by the same Route.

The Company's TOURIST AND EXCURSION PROGRAMME, giving full particulars, will be forwarded free upon application.

TOURIST and WEEK-END EXCURSION TICKETS are also issued from most principal places to ALTON, RUDYARD LAKE (the "Name-place" of Rudyard Kipling), ASHBOURNE (for DOVEDALE), and BUXTON, each Season.

These and other places of great interest, such as—

RUDYARD LAKE—The Windermere of the Midlands—Fishing, Boating, Bathing, Golf. Arrangements can be made for Camping-out in delightfully wooded, sheltered nooks on the borders of the Lake. Apply to Station-master at Rudyard, or to the undersigned.

Hotel Rudyard—Recently Enlarged—Very Comfortable.

WATERHOUSES, for the Caldon Low Limestone Quarries—the happy hunting ground of the geologist.

MANIFOLD VALLEY TOY RAILWAY—2 ft. 6 in. gauge—runs along the Valley of the Manifold to the point where it sinks into the earth to reappear at Ilam, four miles away—the most beautiful scenery in Staffordshire.

LEEK, for Rock Hall, the Roaches and Morridge Hills, and for the Manifold Valley Toy Railway.

TUTBURY, with its Ancient and Historical Castle, Beautiful Church, and Glass Works.

DENSTONE, for Croxden Abbey Ruins, Denstone College, and the Weaver Hills.

CONGLETON, for the Splendid Old Church at Astbury, Moreton Old Hall, Biddulph Grange, The Cloud, The Dane Viaducts, &c.

And also the magnificent Wood, Hill, and River Scenery of the Churnet and Dove Valleys, are easy of access by the "NORTH STAFFORD" Route.

The Public are particularly requested to ask for Tickets by the "NORTH STAFFORD" Route, and to see that such Tickets are supplied to them.

Applications for information as to Traffic for this Route should be made to—

W. D. PHILLIPPS, *General Manager,*

Railway Offices, STOKE-ON-TRENT ; or any of the Company's Agents in the various Towns.

passengers to travel second class were never successful, the only reaction of many travellers being to complain that third class coaches were bare and draughty.

Another handicap to revenue increases was the large number of workmen's weekly tickets, issued at a reduced rate on which compensation for 'injury or otherwise' was limited to £100.

The religious attitudes of shareholders frustrated the development of one area where the directors saw possible traffic growth: the running of Sunday trains to give workers a day out in the country. In Edwardian times, nearly 400 shareholders called for a limit on Sunday excursions.

Economies were frequent and one of the most notable occurred in 1880, when the NSR stopped running to Nottingham to save the £700 it paid to use the Midland station.

Many improvements and additions to the system were made in the Edwardian years. Three stations and a halt opened in the first four years of the century. A new station for Hanley, Waterloo Road, was added to the Loop line in spring 1900, less than half a mile from the town's original station. It was the last station, rather than halt, to open on the Loop, and the first to close, the passenger service being a World War 2 casualty in

1943. Goods were handled at Waterloo Road for another 21 years.

A second station opened, in August 1900, was at Stretton & Clay Mills, further reducing the short distances between Burton branch stations. But the additional stop made no difference to the 6min timings between Rolleston-on-Dove and Horninglow by the Burton-Tutbury local trains.

Consall, a busy village in the Churnet Valley south of Leek, got a station in March 1902, and a fifth intermediate station, Aston-by-Stone, was built on the Stone-Colwich main line in autumn 1904. Two years later — in November 1906 — a new station was built at Fenton to replace its original one, pulled down the day before.

Local services faced increased competition after electric trams replaced steam trams on routes in the heart of the Potteries in 1899. The NSR Deputy Chairman said it was almost impossible to compete with trams because their lines were laid on roads. This meant that tram companies did not have to buy land or meet the operating restrictions which the Board of Trade placed on trains.

The NSR met the challenge by introducing railmotors in May 1905, 'third-class, hand baggage only'. They served stations and eight halts in the Stoke and Newcastle areas. Initial

Left: Railmotor No 1 being tested at Leek Brook Junction in 1905. The railmotors made little impact on traffic because they lacked reserves of power to cope with heavy loads. *LGRP/Bucknall Collection*

Right: Railmotor No 2 in the Churnet Valley. J. W. Walker took many fine photographs of the Knotty, including this study at Oakamoor. *Author's Collection*

Below right: NSR Milk Consignment Note dating from March 1909. *Author's Collection*

routes were soon extended and by 1908 they maintained a 15min service on the Loop line, augmented on local market days.

The rail motors ran over 50,000 miles a year until Grouping, but faced increasing competition from trams which could serve far better the congested towns. They were followed by motorbuses and privately owned cars which, as early as 1908, were modestly but firmly established locally. Hopes of NSR directors that people who usually travelled first class would quickly get tired of riding about in cars and return to the railway were soon dashed.

Yet despite competition, the company was carrying nearly 10 million passengers a year before World War 1. Seven million travelled third class.

To the North Staffordshire Railway Company.

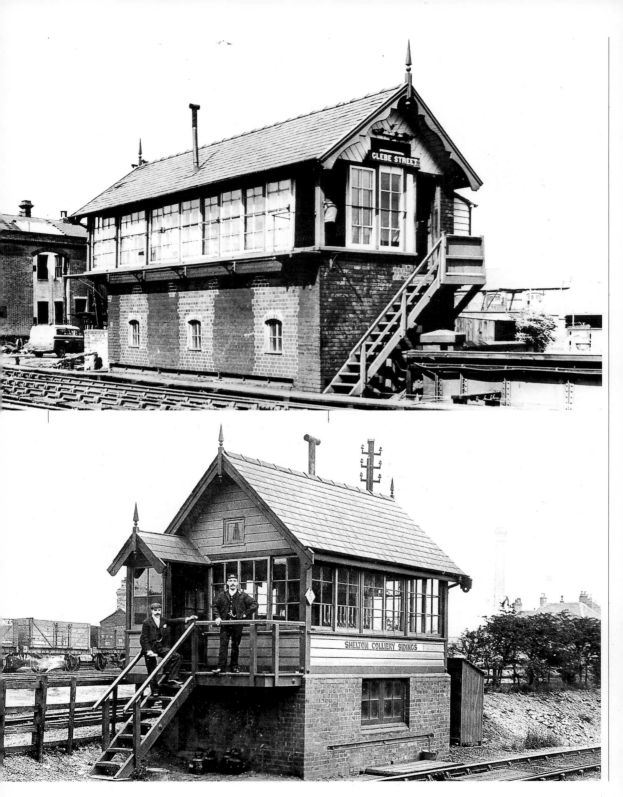

Working the line

Management and men

Staff grew to around 5,000, a number of whom spent their working lives on the line. Outstanding among a group of long-serving senior officers was W. D. Phillipps, who became General Manager in 1882, a Director in 1917 and was still on the Board at the Grouping. The company secretary from 1894, R. E. Pearce, thought his position important enough to warrant having a bell fitted to his home at Stone, so that the signalman could give him enough time to walk to the station with dignity.

NSR discipline was modelled on the LNWR. In 1848 staff were ordered to shave off beards or be dismissed — a rule retained by Euston, although it was relaxed by the NSR in the mid-1860s. Gradually the working week was reduced. In 1866, the hours of drivers were cut — to 72hr! That was when Victorian management thought the labouring classes had more time on their hands than they wanted, even though they were working a six-day week.

The fact that railwaymen were not held in any especial regard by the establishment became obvious after a none-too-serious accident at Stoke station in winter 1872, when an LNWR Manchester-London goods running under clear signals hit the back of an excursion waiting to leave the up platform.

The Inspecting Officer, Lt-Col F. H. Rich, was critical of working between station signalboxes —

and of the men's comfort. They sat in high-back armchairs with glass side windows to look right and left. Colonel Rich noted: 'The signalmen are on duty for 12 hours but I submit it is not desirable that such comfortable means should be provided for the men to go to sleep on duty... if duty hours are too long they should be shortened. If the men are too delicate to perform their duty in a well enclosed and roofed cabin where they are provided with a good fire, they should be invalided and proper men engaged to do the duty.'

Yet despite his recommendation that the seats should be immediately removed, a number survived in use at several boxes, including Kidsgrove Central Junction, Chatterley and Leek Brook Junction. The latter is preserved in the National Railway Museum.

Railwaymen did not always enjoy the sympathy of shareholders. Regretting only a small dividend being paid in 1878, several wanted to know why the NSR had not reduced the wages of drivers, porters and other staff, as the Midland and several other companies had done. The Chairman replied that the NSR had to pay wages no lower than those of neighbouring companies.

Above left: Glebe Street signalbox was at the south end of Stoke station. A turntable was behind the box. It closed in summer 1966. *Author*

Left: Shelton Colliery Sidings box controlled entry to the private sidings from the Loop line between Waterloo Road and Cobridge. Smart, uniformed staff with prominent watch chains and highly-polished black footwear stand on a short balcony beside the entrance shelter. The windows are spotlessly clean. *LGRP*

Right: Before joining the NSR, W. D. Phillipps was LNWR District Superintendent, Manchester. He was so successful in subsequent negotiations for the NSR that the LNWR Chairman, Sir Richard Moon, once remarked: 'We had taught him too much!' *Author's Collection*

There was disagreement between management and men during national unrest among railwaymen. NSR men's demands in winter 1898 were rejected by Sir Thomas Salt (Chairman 1883-1904). He said pay claims would cost at least £40,000 — equal to a 1½% dividend. He contended: 'Of all the workmen in this country, almost the best in their position were those connected with the railway service. They had regular and good employment and good wages.'

The directors felt that a man joining the NSR should feel 'that he may look to remaining with them for the rest of his life'. The Chairman referred to benefits given to the men, including privilege tickets and holidays. There were others. Among the more unusual privileges was that which allowed the wives and families of Caldon Low quarry workers to ride up the incline in empty wagons with their heavily laden shopping baskets, after returning to Froghall by train from Wednesday markets at Leek.

Signals and operation

Just as timetables like Bradshaw's have the power to illustrate, educate and delight, and provide a wealth of information beyond the mainstream, so do track plans. The Signalling Record Society's BR Layout Plans from the John Swift collection covering former NSR lines in the 1950s show detail down to wicket gates — where they were situated and the position of locks.

Despite the complexities of the NSR and the intensive working at its heart, the company never had a major accident. Signalling was very much to the style of the LNWR, with station clocks regulated to its time. Trains were slow. For years, the guards or firemen of trains unable to move at more than 6mph were sent back 800yd and had to follow them at that distance.

A signalman who saw two trains approaching a junction on different lines had to keep signals at danger and let neither pass until he was sure there was no danger of collision.

Passenger trains were always given priority over other traffic; mineral, cattle or ballast trains had to shunt at least 10min before they were scheduled to be overtaken, and then wait until 5min after they had been passed before following. Main lines at stations had to be kept clear for passenger trains, for 10min in advance where practicable.

Block working did not start until 1863 and it was not until 17 years later that one of the busiest junctions between the main line and the Audley line was improved.

Signals were contracted from McKenzie & Holland and many had their characteristic tall, slender posts, topped by finials. Not all were

Above: Elton Crossing Box remained open until the Sandbach branch closed after a derailment in winter 1971. *Ian Allan Library*

brightly lit: one observer described them as almost equalled in brilliance by glow worms on track embankments.

A major improvement of 1883 was the adoption of green for the 'all right' signal.

The NSR became known for its distinctive signalboxes with steeply-sloping roofs and heavy, overhanging eaves. Box names were on cast metal plates attached to the front. The largest box, Stoke, had 51 levers controlling 33 signals and 20 points.

Despite affinities with the LNWR, NSR signalling practice was different in several ways, including block instrument design. LNWR rulebooks had several regulations which NSR engine drivers had to obey. Although the LNWR used only one detonator in foggy weather, NSR drivers were instructed that they 'must act in the same way as when two detonators are exploded'.

NSR drivers had to carry out vacuum brake tests before passing distant signals at principal stations or junctions: Stoke, Crewe Junction (Down), Burton NS Junction (Up), Colwich (Up), Macclesfield (Hibel Road), Macclesfield Central (Up) and Rocester (Up).

Regulations affecting NSR operations over the GWR were contained in a 13-page Appendix to the Working Time Book. It was issued from the headquarters at Stoke station in January 1915. One section dealt with regulations for getting two passenger trains into Market Drayton Up platform together 'when such an operation cannot be avoided'.

Right: Uttoxeter was the scene of two spectacular accidents. A nosedive by a Class E 0-6-0 almost demolished a signal gantry. The NSR Cowan & Sheldon 1899 steam crane begins recovery, watched by bowler-hatted 'gaffers'. *T. G. Hall*

Below: In the second Uttoxeter accident, the front end of Class C 2-4-0 No 14 was badly buckled in a station derailment. The van was embedded in the tender. *LGRP*

There was always concern about safety at level crossings, especially in the densely populated areas at the heart of the Potteries. After two boys were killed at Longport, the company provided an under-bridge because the crossing was busy, being used by 800 people a day. But when the directors refused to make a similar improvement at Stoke station, the Commissioner of Police reported the company to the Board of Trade.

Accidents were due to a variety of causes. In summer 1861, a young girl was killed and eight other passengers slightly hurt when an evening local from Colwich broke a tyre at Hixon. The following year, the driver, fireman and guard of a Burton-Stoke local train were killed when it left the rails and ran into a field. The sobriety of the driver was questioned, but a more likely cause of the accident was the instability of the engine.

The attitude of NSR management was that accidents involving passengers could not be 'expected' but those involving staff could. The point was well illustrated after an LNWR express from Manchester ran into an NSR mineral train at Sideway, killing the LNWR driver in January 1885. The NSR Chairman remarked that two men had made a mistake and added that it was absolutely impossible to prevent accidents altogether as long as they had to deal with the human agency. The Board of Trade disputed the Chairman's findings, saying signalling — not men — was at fault.

The Inspector's report led to schemes for making signalling safer, with new types of interlocking points and telegraph instruments. Nationally, a number were put forward by patentees, engineers and superintendents of railway companies.

Other collisions between LNWR and NSR trains included the derailment of the noon Manchester-London express at Longport in 1871, after a shunting rope was left stretched across the main line. Passengers escaped serious injury.

Shunting poles were introduced by the NSR in 1885. The Chairman claimed they were a step towards greater safety while admitting that there was still some danger to men. But, he contended, the poles were a convenience which reduced the dangers to shunters. Men could marshal trains quicker by using them, coupling up to 40 wagons in 4-5min.

Staff who became tired while working long hours were involved in accidents. Some of the longest spells were worked by gatemen, who had to be on duty at least 30min before the passage of the first morning train and continue until the last of the day had run.

Passenger regulations

Timetables warned passengers that horses and carriages had to be at stations at least 30min before departure of trains carrying vehicles for them, and these had to be ordered at least 24hr earlier.

Commercial travellers, equestrian performers and theatre and operatic parties could take with them, free of charge, 'a quantity of their business effects' amounting to 3cwt if they were travelling first class; 2cwt if they had second class tickets

Left: In a quest to improve express passenger services, four 4-4-0s of a new design were built at Stoke in 1910, the year J. W. Walker photographed No 170 at Uttoxeter. The leading vehicle is a horsebox. *Author's Collection*

Below: All passenger services stopped at Stoke, though few began or ended journeys there. One of the handsome 'K' 4-4-2Ts — No 46 of 1911 — heads a working carrying express headcode. The first vehicle is labelled 'Fruit and Milk Traffic'. *LPC*

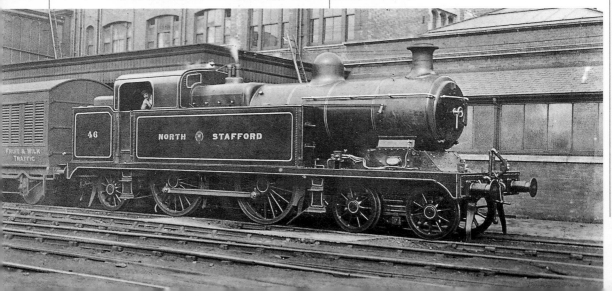

and 1½cwt if they were booked third class. *Bona fide* emigrants could travel with 1cwt of personal luggage.

Doors of station parcel offices were closed 15min before train departures. From such offices parcels weighing up to 14lb were delivered free 'within the usual delivery boundary of most NSR stations'.

Fares and tickets

The NSR made an early impact on ticketing practices of the railways of Britain by piloting through the Railway Clearing House in 1852, a scheme to replace cyphers on tickets with information on routes, useful to passengers and ticket collectors. The change was radical for it meant placing the initials of the issuing company on the front of tickets.

Friendly relations with Euston led to the introduction in 1866 of annual season tickets from stations in the Potteries to those on the LNWR at that company's rates.

The NSR directors were angered in 1868 when they learnt that free train passes were issued to some local schoolchildren. The scheme was stopped at once, partly because the NSR could not afford to lose any source of revenue. A decade later, the highest adult local fare was under 10 shillings and the average was only nine old pence.

Fare dodging was a problem from the earliest days, but staff were warned about the difficulties and dangers when offenders were caught. The 1865 Rule Book and those issued subsequently, warned staff to use the power of detention with great caution — and to 'convey' a person before a magistrate with as little delay as possible. The directors were concerned because passengers frequently travelled unintentionally beyond the station to which they had paid a fare — 'or even did so against their wish'.

In 1911, boys of Market Drayton Grammar School were given special cheap fares; the NSR, which lost revenue from the scheme, hoped it would attract builders to the district. To tempt people to live in rural areas, monthly contracts were issued to country stations from those in the Potteries and Newcastle. Golfers were offered special fares to entice them to play on the NSR course at Rudyard.

Train services

Initially because of poor brakes, maximum speeds were slow. Special passenger trains were limited to 25mph; goods and ballast trains and light engines to 20mph 'without distinct orders to the contrary'.

The proud and independent NSR never felt humbled by the most important and fastest expresses using its metals belonging to another company. Indeed, it enjoyed the prestige of its locomotives hauling some of the three daily Manchester (London Road)-Euston expresses over the first 37½ miles to Stoke.

In 1897, the year of Queen Victoria's Diamond Jubilee, the noon departure from London Road was often in the charge of an NSR locomotive allowed 65min to Stoke. A variety were used including small tanks sometimes mistaken for a station pilot! But the sturdy NSR designs could pull heavy expresses, although southbound from Macclesfield they had to be banked to the Moss by an NSR locomotive.

At Stoke, 4min were allowed for an LNWR tender locomotive to take over for the run to Euston with arrival at 4.15pm. The expresses were the most prestigious trains to call at Stoke and while local trains were crammed two or three along the platform, they occupied the whole length. The Manifold authors noted that 'a preliminary ceremonial hush settled over Stoke station when they were due and the top-hatted stationmaster turned out for the noon to London'.

NSR timetables stated that the Londons did not convey horses and private carriages. As an incentive to strict timekeeping, the company faced a penalty of £1 for every minute lost while on its metals.

The expresses supplemented the NSR's own stopping service of several daily trains between Manchester and Stoke. On Saturdays there were cheap half-day excursion bookings to Manchester, with the last train not returning from London Road until 11.3pm, calling at Longsight 5min later to pick up passengers from Belle Vue pleasure gardens.

The LNWR utilised part of the NSR for a Euston-Ashbourne-Buxton service. Buxton portions were slipped at Nuneaton from a morning Welsh express (through coaches to Aberystwyth and Pwllheli), and a through coach was attached to Euston expresses at Rugby in late afternoon. Buxton journeys took some 5hr. On the NSR the through coaches were worked on stopping trains.

An unusual feature of Stoke-Birmingham (New Street) services was that those routed via Colwich were worked by NSR locomotives (especially 4-4-2Ts in later years), while those via Stafford were hauled by LNWR locomotives.

The character of NSR local services was well summed up by Phillipps in 1899: 'Most of our runs are so short that the drivers are afraid to put on much speed for fear of running 20 or 30 miles on to somebody else's line before they stop.'

The hub was always Stoke; the system had no junction to rival it. In Edwardian days, it handled 230 daily services. During the busiest period in the

For other Trains between Stoke and Harecastle, see pages 6 and 7.

LONDON, BIRMINGHAM (SOUTH STAFFORD STATIONS), STAFFORD, STOKE, MACCLESFIELD, STOCKPORT, AND MANCHESTER.

Mls.	STATIONS.	WEEK-DAYS.														
			am			am	am	am	am		am	pm	pm	noon		
	L. and N. W. Railway.															
	London(Euston) *dep.*	...	...	...	...	5 15	...	7 30	...	...	9 30	...	...	12 0	...	...
	Rugby	...	...	...	...	7 12	7 18	9 44	...	...	11 30	...	...	1 50	...	...
	Nuneaton	...	...	...	...	7 34	8 10	10 5	...	...	11 17	...	...	1 15	...	...
	Tamworth	...	...	...	...	7 51	8 40	10 28	...	...	11 35	..	...	1 40	...	...
	Lichfield	...	...	...	am	8 4	9 12	10 40	...	...	11 52	...	...	2 35	...	...
	Birmingham	...	5 50	...	6 5	7 20	9 5	9 50	9B15	...	11 35	12 20	12 5	...	...	...
	Dudley	...	...	...	...	7 28	9 10	10 5	8B40	...	11 10	12 20	12 20	HC	...	...
	Walsall	...	...	...	6 43	7 15	8 55	9 45	9B40	...	11 30	1 2	12 42		...	...
	Wolverhampton	...	6 40	...	6 20	7 50	9 36	10 35	8B30	...	12 1	12 30	1 25		...	...
	Cannock	...	...	...	7 2	...	8 40	9 57	9B57	...	10 35	1 27	...		...	...
	Rugeley Junction	...	...	...	7 25	8 24	9 27	10 20	10B20	...	11 40	1 55	...		...	...
	Shrewsbury	...	...	...	...	7 40	7 40	...	...	...	11 40	...	12 40		...	...
	Wellington	...	...	...	...	7 59	7 59	...	...	...	12 6	...	12 55		...	...
Mls in Staffo'd		mrn	mrn	mrn	mrn	mrn	mrn	HC mrn	mrn	aft	aft	aft	aft	Express London to Manchester	aft	aft
	STAFFORD *dep.*	...	7 25	...	...	8 56	10 10	11 14	...	...	1 3	...	2 25		...	...
	GREAT BRIDGEFORD	...	7 31	...	...	9 2	...	...	...	...	..	...	...		...	...
5¼	NORTON B'DGE *for E'shall*	...	7 37	...	...	9 10	10 23	...	...	...	1 13	...	2 35		...	...
	Colwich Line.															
	COLWICH *dep.*	...	...	...	8 25	...	...	Express	11B15	*Saturd'ys only*	...	2 5	...		...	...
	GREAT HAYWOOD	...	...	...	8 29	...	...		11B19		...	2 9	...		...	...
	HIXON	...	...	...	8 34	...	...		11B24		...	2 14	...		...	...
	WESTON (Ingestre)	...	...	...	8 38	...	...		11B28		...	2 19	...		...	...
	SANDON	...	...	...	8 44	...	...		11B34		...	2 26	...		...	...
9¼	STONE Junction *dep.*	...	7 45	8 15	8 53	9 17	10 31	11 30	11 43	...	1 20	2 36	2 43	...	...	4 0
11½	BARLASTON (Tittensor)	...	7 51	8 21	8 59	9 22	10 37	...	11 49	...	1 26		2 49	...	...	4 6
13¼	TRENTHAM	...	7 57	8 27	9 4	9 27	10 44	...	11 54	...	1 32	...	2 55	...	...	4 13
16	**STOKE** *arr.*	...	8 3	8 33	9 10	9 32	10 50	11 42	12 ‡0	...	1 38	...	3 2	3 18	...	4‡19
	STOKE *dep.*	7 20	8 6	...		9 50	11 0	11 44	12 18	*1 40*	1 50	..		3 22	3 25	4 30
17	ETRURIA (Basford)	7 25	8 10	...		9 54	11 5	...	12 22	*1 44*	1 54	...	...	...	...	4 34
18¾	LONGPORT	7 30	8 16	...		9 59	11 10	...	12 27	*1 49*	1 59	...	...		3 31	4 39
20¼	CHATTERLEY	7 35	D	...		10 4	11 15	Express	...	*1 54*	2 4	...	...	Express	...	4 44
22	HARECASTLE (Kidsgrove)	7 40	8 23	...		10 9	11 23		12 34	*1 59*	2 9	...	...		3 37	4 49
	HARECASTLE *dep.*	7 43	...	...		...	...		12 40	...	*3S20*	...	...		To Crewe	To Crewe
	LAWTON	7 48	...	...		...	...		12 45	...	*3S25*	...	...			
	SANDBACH (Whe'lck) *a.*	7 58	...	...		...	...		12 55	...	*3S35*	...	...			
24½	MOW COP (Scholar Green)	...	8 29	...		10 15	11 29	...	...	*2 5*	2 16	...	...	...	...	...
27¾	CONGLETON	...	8 36	...		10 22	11 36	...	...	*2 12*	2 23	...	...	...	...	...
31	NORTH RODE Junction	...	...	...		10 30	11 43	...	...	*2 20*	2 32	...	...	...	...	...
35¾	MACCLESFIELD (Central)	...	8 50	...		10 40	11 53		...	*2 30*	2 41	...	...	...	...	...
	BUXTON *via* M'dlewood	...	10 22	...		12 54	3 17	3 17	...	...	5 9	...	...	5 9	...	...
36	MACCLESFIELD(H.R.) *arr.*	...	8 52	...		10 42	11 55	12 13	...	*2 32*	2 42	...	...	3 48	...	...
	L. & N.W. Railway															
	Stockport *arr.*	...	9 18	...		11 9		12 33	...	...	3 17	...	...	4 10	...	...
	Manchester*	...	9 35	...		11 21		12 45	...	...	3 29	..	...	4 20	...	...
	Huddersfield	...	11 3	...		12 37		2 20	...	...	5 34	...	...	5 34	...	...
	Leeds (New Station)	...	11 35	...		1 8		3 11	...	...	6 2	...	...	6 2	...	...
	L. & Y. Bradford	...	12 18	...		2 22		3 25	...	...	6 43	...	...	6 43	..	...

B—*Tuesdays and Saturdays only.*

D—Calls on *Tuesdays.*

S—*Saturdays only.*

‡—Passengers change at Stoke.

*—London Road.

H C—Horses and private carriages are not conveyed by this Train.

For other Trains between Stoke and Harecastle, see pages 6 ahd 7.

LONDON, BIRMINGHAM, (SOUTH STAFFORD STATIONS),
STAFFORD, STOKE,
MACCLESFIELD, STOCKPORT, AND MANCHESTER.

STATIONS						WEEK-DAYS.								SUNDAYS.				
			pm		pm	pm	pm	pm		pm			am	pm	pm		
L. & N. W. RAILWAY. London (Eus.)d.	...	...	1 30	...	...	4 0	2 45	4 10	..	6 30	...	..	10 0	...	...	..
Rugby	...	...	3 20	...	...	5 50	5 5	6 2	..	8 23	...	..	12 18	...	...	..
Nuneaton........	...	...	3 43	...	...	5 28	5 28	5 28	..	8 46	...	..	12 41	...	...	..
Tamworth........	...	...	3 16	...	...	5 54	5 54	6 36	..	8 37	...	..	1 5	...	...	..
Lichfield	...	...	4 11	...	...	6 33	6 6	6 6	..	8 48	...	..	1 17	...	...	..
Birmingham	...	...	3 40	4 40	...		5 50	5 20	..	8 40	...	8 45	12 45	...	5 10	..
Dudley..........	...	...	3 45	4 48	...	HC	5 35	5 30	..	8 45	...	9 0	12 45	...	5 10	..
Walsall.........	...	...	3 40	4 33	5 13		5 30	6 5	..	8 25	...		11 50	...	5 48	..
Wolverhampton ..	...	...	4 8		5 13		6 13	5 35	..	9 10	...	9 32	1 18	...	5 0	..
Cannock.........	...	...	3 23	...	...		5 32	6 26	..	8 25	...		10 27	...	6 8	..
Rugeley Junction....	...	...	3 47	...	...		6 26	7 7	..	9 5	...		1 32	...	6 30	..
Shrewsbury	...	...	2 25	...	...		5 40	...	..	8 0	...		...	4 30	...	..
Wellington	...	...	2 41	...	...		5 55	...	..	8 28	..		...	4 57	...	..
	aft	aft	aft	aft	aft		aft	aft	aft	aft	aft	mrn	mrn	aft	aft	aft	aft
STAFFORD........ dep.	...	...	4 50	...	5 45		7 0	...	..	9 50			10 0	2 15	6 45	...	..
GREAT BRIDGEFORD ..	...	...	...		C		7 6	...	..	...			...	...	...	...	..
NRTON BGE for Ecclshall	...	...	5 0		5 57		7 12	...	..	10 0			10 10	2 25	6 55	...	..
COLWICH .. dep.		...	...	...	...		...	7 13	..	...			...	...	...	7 10	..
GREAT HAYWO'D		...	...	...	...		...	7 17	..	...			...	...	...	7 15	..
HIXON.........		...	...	...	...		...	7 22	..	...			...	...	...	7 21	..
WESTON (Ingestr)		...	...	...	...		...	7 26	..	...			...	...	...	7 26	..
SANDON		...	...	...	...		...	7 32	..	...			...	...	...	7 32	..
STONE Junction ..dep.			5 8	6 5	...		7 20	7 42	..	10 8	1130		10 18	2 34	7 3	7 43	9 10
BARLASTON (Tittensor)			5 14	6 11	...		7 26	7 48	..	10 14	...		10 24	2 40	7 9	7 50	9 16
TRENTHAM			5 20	6 17	...		7 32	7 54	..	10 21			10 29	2 46	7 15	7 57	9 21
STOKE { arr		5 3	5 26	6 23	7 14		7 38	8 0	..	10 28	1142		10 35	2 55	7 25	8 8	9 30
{ dep	5 4	5 6	5 32			7 17		8 5	8 25	11 5		8 5	10 45	3 0	7 30	8 28	
ETRURIA (Basford) ..	5 4			6 6	...			8 9		HC		8 10	10 50	3 5	7 34	8 33	
LONGPORT	5 9		5 38	6 12	...			8 14	8 32	11 12		8 15	10 55	3 11	7 39	8 39	
CHATTERLEY	5 14			6 17	...			8 19				8 20	11 0	3 17	7 44	8 45	
HAREC'STLE (Kidsgrov)	5 19	5A31	5 45	6 45	...			8 24	8 39	11 19		8 29	11 5	3 23	7 50	8 52	
HARECASTLE ..dep	..	...	5 50	..	...			...	9S20			..	...	...	...	...	
LAWTON	..	...	5 55	..	...			...	9S25			..	...	...	...	...	
SANDBACH(Whe'lck)a	..	...	6 5	..	...			...	9S35			..	...	...	...	...	
MOW COP (Scholar Gn.)	5 25	D	...	6 52	...			8 30				8 35	...	3 31	7 56	8 59	
CONGLETON	5 33	5 40	5 56	6 58	...	G		8 37				8 42	...	3 39	8 4	9 8	
NORTH RODE Junction	5 42		D	...	...			8 46				8 50	...	3 47		9 17	
MACCLESFIELD(Central)	5 51		6 9	...	...			8 56				8 59	...	3 58	8 23		
BUXTON via M'wood	7 11	...	8 Y2	...	...	9H35	11F52					..	7H23	...	...	...	
MACCLESFIELD(H.R.)ar	5 53	...	6 10	...	...		7 43	8 58				9 0	...	4 0	8 25	9 27	
L. & N. W. Railway Stockport ..arr.	6 31	...	6 31	...	...		8 3	9 39				9 35	...	5 27	8 48	1013	..
Manchester*..	6 43	...	6 43	...	...		8 15	10 1				9 58	...	5 52	9 0	1036	..
Huddersfield ..	8 6	...	8 6	...	...		9 30	1 50				..	...	8 5	...	...	..
L. & Y. Leeds†	8 50	...	8 50	...	...		10 20	5 47				..	...	9 2	...	...	..
Bradford....	9 25	...	9 25	...	...		10 30	6 45				..	...	10 4	...	...	..

A—Kidsgrove Station.   C—Calls to pick up Passengers.   D—Calls on *Saturdays*.

F—*Via* Stockport, L. & N.W., *Thursdays & Saturdays only*.   G—Stops to set down from
London only, on notice being given to the Guard at Euston or Willesden.

H—*Via* Stockport, L. & N. W.   S—*Saturdays only*.

Y—*Mondays, Tuesdays, Wednesdays and Fridays only. Via Stockport*, L.&N.W.

‡—Passengers change at Stoke.   *—London Road.   †—New Station.

H C—Horses and private carriages are not conveyed by this Train.

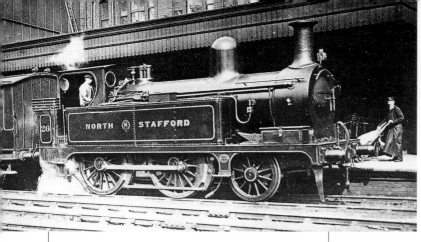

evening rush, over 30 trains an hour were diagrammed into the two main platforms and the north Down bay.

Most timings changed little over the years and many trains ran to timings laid down when lines were opened or soon afterwards. In 1897, Stoke-Norton Bridge trains, which generally ran through to Stafford, were still taking 25min to cover 11 miles with three intermediate stops.

Operating flexibility was helped by all NSR passenger services running independently, timetables warning passengers that there was no connection between them.

Loop trains were so frequent that workers often caught them to get home for lunch. No wonder the company was once commended for being among railways which had met and stimulated a demand for frequent and effective suburban and inter-district services. Loop trains ran every few minutes from 6am until after 11pm: more than 50 in each direction. The most intensive service was through the Potteries' heart between Tunstall, five miles north of Stoke, and Normacot, three miles south.

The LNWR regarded Macclesfield-Colwich as the NSR main line, but NSR timetables gave preference to the Crewe to Stoke, Uttoxeter, Burton and Derby service. It had five stopping trains each way, reduced to one on Sundays. Some ran through to Derby and others formed part of NSR local services to and from Manchester London Road. They used the LNWR main line from Macclesfield, rather than the Macclesfield, Bollington & Marple, to serve Stockport. Up trains were allowed 40min from Manchester to Macclesfield (Hibel Road) and 1hr 25min for the 32 miles through the valley to Uttoxeter. Overall time to Derby was almost one hour longer.

Many children living in the valley went to school by train. At the age of 89, Mr J. E. Coates recalled catching the 8.9am from Oakamoor while he was a pupil at Uttoxeter Grammar School from 1896 to 1901. The 9½-mile journey then took 25min. 'The carriages were without corridors, lighted (sic) by dim oil lamps and heated by battered footwarmers.'

Mr Coates' affection for the Knotty prompted him to buy an Oakamoor station sign — 'enamelled iron, black on yellow ground, as it was when the line was abandoned'.

The Churnet line also carried a five-mile local service between Leek and Rushton, on which Rudyard Lake and Cliffe Park halt both served the lake. After Nationalisation, the London Midland Region recognised the recreational attractions of Rudyard Lake by adding its name to the timetable heading.

Connections were made at Leek between Churnet Valley trains and a stopping service to Stoke, on which Bucknall & Northwood station was shown as a station for Hanley — the main shopping centre of the Potteries. Passengers who read a footnote warning that Hanley was a mile away, probably decided it was more comfortable and convenient to reach Hanley by changing to the Loop line at Stoke, although the journey was four miles longer.

Besides being the junction for the Churnet and Ashbourne lines, Uttoxeter was among the busiest NSR stations outside the Potteries, because it was also used by six weekday Great Northern trains between Stafford, Derby and Nottingham.

The NSR Burton branch had eight daily trains to and from Tutbury. The 5½-mile route had an intermediate station at Rolleston-on-Dove and calls were made at Burton Horninglow and Station Street, stations only a mile apart.

The 'Tutbury Jennie' was often hauled in later years by Midland 0-4-4Ts. Deep in memory is a Sunday journey on the 11.15am from Tutbury just after Nationalisation, when the branch encapsulated the spirit and fascination of run-down, if not doomed, branch passenger services. Yet, like so much of the NSR, it had a value on which it survived long after the onset of bus, car

and lorry competition, to which it did not succumb until summer 1960.

West of Stoke, Newcastle-Market Drayton services and those over the Audley branch to Kidsgrove were detailed in the same timetable, subheaded 'with through service to Great Western stations'. On alternate Tuesdays, NSR Market Drayton trains were extended six miles south over the GWR Nantwich-Wellington secondary route, so that people going to market in the village of Hodnet did not have a 2hr wait for a GWR connection.

The Stoke-Market Drayton branch was busy at the eastern, industrial Potteries end; quiet to the west where it ran through sparsely populated north Shropshire. Four or five trains ran on weekdays between Stoke and Market Drayton, but others terminated at Silverdale and Keele.

Three daily passenger trains over the Audley line were pathed between 17 Stoke-Newcastle local trains; a service maintained at that intensity for many years.

Market days always boosted traffic. Hodnet was among a number of small villages some distance from the Potteries to which the NSR issued third class market tickets. They were restricted to stated trains for outward journeys, but passengers could return home 'by ordinary stopping train'. They could also carry, free, baskets or other packages containing up to 28lb of eggs, butter, fruit or other market produce on market days, but only at their own risk. Market Drayton and Wellington were among 24 places to which market tickets were issued.

Numerous small alterations were being made constantly to timetables. A few trains were accelerated, many were cancelled in winter, especially Sunday trains between the Potteries and surrounding country areas, including the Churnet Valley.

During the hunting season, hunting contract tickets, first class only, were 'issued under special regulations' and some services were altered to meet the needs of their holders: the 9.27am Stoke-Stone was one example. When hunts were meeting in adjacent areas, horseboxes were added to the formation and the train extended to either Sandon or Norton Bridge.

Excursions: coast and country

For years the people of the Potteries loved the North Wales seaside resorts, especially Llandudno, backclothed by the mountains of Snowdonia. Llandudno became the terminus of summer holiday expresses, which were virtually extended Derby-Crewe services.

The 11am departure from Derby (NSR) was normally made up of three coaches from that station, one from Nottingham MR and another from Nottingham GNR. A sixth coach, from Burton, was added at Uttoxeter. At Stoke, the express detached a coach for the Cambrian Coast. The express ran nonstop through Crewe, stopping at Beeston Castle, Chester, Rhyl, Colwyn Bay and Llandudno, not reached until mid-afternoon (2.50pm). The working was balanced by an LNWR service, which did call at Crewe. Running powers used on the Derby-Llandudno link of 118½ miles meant that NSR stock — locomotives and carriages — ran further than was possible on their own system.

Numerous excursions starting from Stoke ran at holiday times, especially during August Wakes Weeks. Besides those to North Wales coastal resorts, tourist tickets were issued to Fylde line stations; Fleetwood, Lytham and Blackpool throughout the year. Those to a number of other places were discontinued in the winter.

Mr Coates remembered that excursions from the Churnet Valley often started about 4am. 'A favourite was to Belle Vue, Manchester: zoo, brass band contests, etc.' Many railway excursions ran

to the Churnet Valley from considerable distances for the week-long Alton Towers Fête.

He also saw the building of the Manifold Valley Light Railway 'and used to enjoy expeditions it afforded to this lovely valley'. The light railway ran extra services connecting with popular summer afternoon excursions from crowded local towns.

Goods and mineral traffic

The volume of NSR goods and mineral traffic was immense for such a small company. The novelist Arnold Bennett immortalised the Loop line, but there was little romantic about goods and mineral trains, which kept it prosperous. Traffic was diverse. While the district was rich in iron and coal, the clay and other materials used by some 400 potteries, large and small, (most with their own distinctively shaped bottle kilns) were brought from other parts of Britain. Around the turn of the century, Baedeker guides noted: 'in every direction rise chimneys, furnaces, warehouses and drying-houses'.

In three decades traffic almost doubled, until by 1913 the NSR was handling over 1¾ million tons of goods, nearly four million tons of coal, coke and patent fuel and over two million tons of other minerals. Much of the traffic originated on the system.

China and earthenware were a useful source of traffic and over 150,000 tons carried in 1913 represented five-sixths of the entire production in Britain. The NSR had to carry this easily-breakable traffic at its own risk and claims sometimes reached a fifth of net receipts.

Another specialist traffic for which the NSR competed keenly was wines and spirits, which it stored in its own bonded warehouses at Hanley.

The backbone of the NSR goods traffic was its express goods services between Nottingham,

Burton, Derby, Leicester and Liverpool and Manchester, with connections to Eastern England, Chester, Birkenhead, North Wales, Lancashire and Northern England. This widely-advertised network was created only through the exercise of running powers over the LNWR, Midland, GNR and GWR. Some covered only short distances, like those by which the GWR allowed the NSR to run goods trains to Wellington in return for working into Stoke over the Market Drayton branch.

The NSR had goods collection and delivery teams and agents at a number of towns and villages outside the Potteries, notably Burton, where there were three agents — more than anywhere else — including one for canal traffic. At Derby, the NSR generated traffic through passenger and goods agents.

Private trains

The NSR did not handle all the goods traffic that ran within the industrial heart of the Potteries, for it encouraged private firms to run their own trains over its lines. In a detailed study, Dr Hollick classified them as unofficial and official. He recorded the anger of NSR directors in 1852 when they were told that the Shelton Iron Co had recently run its locomotive from Etruria to Wheelock and back without prior consent. The board said such an unofficial working was not to happen again!

Official workings included local shunting and main line workings. They were far from being haphazard operations, because private company drivers had to pass NSR rule examinations.

Dr Hollick found that: 'The NSR had no objection to the numbers of private trains that roamed up and down the Biddulph Valley and other lines; they paid toll for their passage, so that was all right. The LMSR had other ideas; their opposition, and the depression, got rid of them'.

Locomotives, Sheds and Rolling Stock

At Grouping, the NSR handed over to the LMS 197 locomotives and three steam railmotors. The locomotives belonged to a number of classes because the company built or acquired from private builders small batches as traffic and economic conditions changed. The policy gave the company a host of interesting locomotive designs.

The largest were four Class G 4-4-0s, a type new to the company when they were built at Stoke in 1910 by the Locomotive Superintendent John Henry Adams. They were designed especially for the Llandudno service and had tenders which could carry enough coal for the round trip, to avoid having to buy it from the LNWR. Class F 0-6-4Ts were occasionally used and from 1911-12 the handsome Class K 4-4-2Ts, basically a tank version of the 4-4-0s.

Both types were among several locomotive classes diagrammed for handling the tightly-timed LNWR midday Manchester-Euston expresses as far as Stoke, where they were taken over by LNWR locomotives, which were the biggest and most powerful to run over NSR metals before Grouping. Other NSR types used on the Eustons were 0-6-0s and, from 1916, Class F tanks.

NSR locomotives proved so sturdy that in the 15 years up to Grouping only 25 were added, a factor which may have led to an early LMS decision to stop locomotive building at Stoke Works. Only four locomotives were completed between Grouping and closure in December 1926, when staff were transferred mainly to Crewe Works, others moving to Derby.

Stoke Locomotive, Carriage & Wagon Works occupied no more than 12 acres and the sole rail access was a spur off the Leek branch, yet they were efficient, busy and innovative. Employees grew to nearly 900, with almost 500 in the locomotive section. In early Victorian days, development was slow and it was not until the late 1860s that they were equipped for locomotive construction.

Below: Among the earliest locomotives was a 2-2-2T No 65, built in 1848 and acquired by the NSR the following year. It was rebuilt as a 2-2-2 well tank in 1859 and became NSR No 3. *IAL/Bucknall Collection*

The first locomotives which the NSR owned were standard designs from private builders. Of 43 locomotives ordered in February 1847, all but one were delivered in 1848-9. Records show that six arrived at Stoke 'under steam' from Norton Bridge on 15 March 1848.

Some designs were primitive and faulty. Samuel Parker Bidder, General Manager 1848-53, favoured Stephenson Patent long-boiler locomotives and ordered 2-4-0s with all their wheels, including 5ft 6in drivers, in front of the firebox. Outside cylinders exacerbated the design fault and made them unsteady above 20-25mph. Yet all but six of the first 33 passenger locomotives were built to this arrangement. The early fleet was augmented by five second-hand locomotives bought from contractors building the lines.

Performance slowly improved and in 1859-61 the original engines were converted from coke to coal fuel, using brick arch fireboxes which gave better combustion.

When a new General Manager, Percy Morris, began a 13-year reign in 1863, he called for an outside consultant's report. It described the stock as 'a parcel of long-boilered locomotives'.

Nearly 50 locomotives were reconstructed after being condemned as unsuited to traffic. The work was supervised by James Johnson, the resident engineer with locomotive responsibilities. He was the father of Samuel Waite Johnson who was to achieve fame as the Locomotive Superintendent of the Midland Railway. James Johnson's reputation was not so high and after he left Stoke in 1870, the Chairman accused him of doing unpopular things. He claimed he had 'queer views and attached fireboxes not suited to the district, which had to be removed at great expense'.

A motley collection of 2-4-0s, 0-6-0s and Kitson singles was inherited by Johnson's successor, Thomas Weatherburn Dodds, inventor of Dodds' wedge motion. He immediately met an urgent need for goods engines, building two of conventional design at Stoke Works in 1871 and ordering 16 more, fitted with wedge motion, from private builders.

For passenger needs, Dodds designed inside-frame 2-4-0s with 6ft 6in drivers, the largest on the system, and wedge motion. Two more under construction were hastily modified because of an 1873 accident, when a light engine was unable to

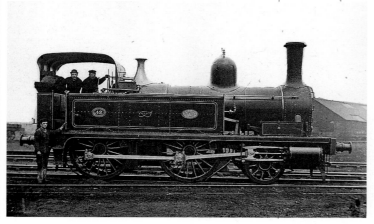

Left: No 27 was built as a 2-2-2 by Sharp Brothers in 1848. It was rebuilt as a 2-4-0 in 1867 and survived until 1883. *Ian Allan Library*

Below left: Outside cylinder 2-4-0T No 42 of 1874 was one of a class which became noted for useful work on the Loop line. *LPC*

Above right: An unusual Robert Stephenson design of 1862 was an 0-6-0ST, numbered either 67 or 68. It is seen at Stoke. *IAL/Bucknall Collection*

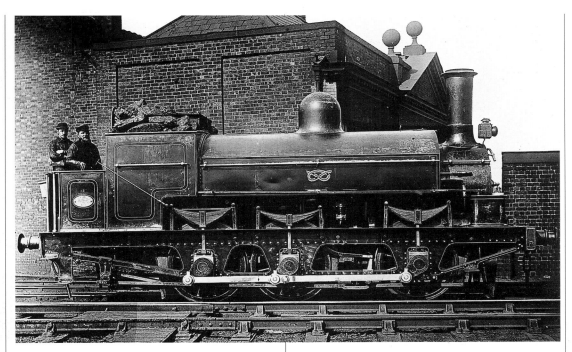

get clear of a runaway train at Lawton Junction because its wedge motion jammed at the crucial moment. Wedge slipping and jamming were common and sometimes locomotives could only be restarted by placing a pinch bar under the wheels.

The débâcle led to a change of policy and Dodds departed in acrimony. The post of Locomotive Superintendent was then created and filled by Robert Angus, whose practical management had kept all the early locomotives running. He replaced all wedge motions with Stephenson valve gear.

C. Clare took over from Angus in 1876 and although his term only lasted until his death seven years later, he was remembered for his efficient rebuilding work. New construction at Stoke was concentrated on tanks for growing local passenger services. Clare also built two 2-4-0 tender engines named after the Chairman and Deputy Chairman.

Because of their rarity, NSR locomotives had the power to rekindle the memories of their admirers half a century later. Hugh Oliver, an NSR historian, recalled catching the 11.19am from Denstone, where he was at college during World War 1, to Uttoxeter several times when it was pulled by *Colin Minton Campbell*. 'I was thrilled to be behind a named NSR locomotive,' he wrote years later.

Clare was succeeded by Luke Longbottom, who was to remain in office for 20 years and become the longest serving Locomotive Superintendent. He altered locomotive livery and placed the Staffordshire Knot emblem on tender or tank sides and on the large splashers of passenger engines.

By the mid-1890s some locomotives were incapable of handling heavier trains. Longbottom's remedy was to fit larger boilers, although they were restricted in size to avoid major modifications to several classes.

The first class to have larger boilers was one of 0-6-0 goods locomotives — the first built at Stoke for 19 years and the first tender engines for 12 years, reflecting the popularity of tank locomotives. Rebuilding with larger boilers continued until 1917. The programme made Stoke Works so busy that for the first time for 15 years, private firms were given orders when more 0-6-0 tender engines were needed in 1900. Because of big increases in train loads nationally, private firms had full order-books and the NSR took six 0-6-0s which the Furness Railway had ordered earlier from Nasmyth Wilson of Patricroft, Manchester, but did not require. Four veterans were bought from the LNWR.

The NSR began 1903 with 177 locomotives forming no less than 17 classes. Additionally, there were three narrow gauge 0-4-0STs working the 3ft 6in lines in Caldon Low quarries.

The start of the Edwardian era brought a considerable improvement in the power and

Left: Another early oddity was No 2, converted from a Sharp Brothers 2-2-2 tender design of 1848 into its final form as a saddle tank at Stoke Works in 1881. It was withdrawn in 1891. *LPC*

Centre left: Another early locomotive, No 16, was a Kitson 2-2-2 of 1848. It was rebuilt at Stoke in 1869. *IAL/Bucknall Collection*

Below: Many NSR locomotives were admired for their sturdy, workmanlike appearance. No 74 of Class E was one of two built at Stoke in 1871. Another 10 were delivered from Vulcan Foundry the following year. *LPC*

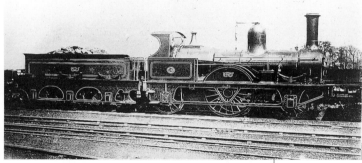

Below right: Another oddity was 2-4-0 No 19 of 1872, fitted with T. W. Dodds' troublesome wedge motion. The driving wheels of 6ft 6in were then the largest on the system. The cab had side windows which could be raised and lowered like those of carriages. *LPC*

Above: No 116 was among eight 0-6-0s built at Sharp Stewart in 1873-4. With only one exception they were in service until after World War 1. *LPC*

Right: Class C 2-4-0 No 55 was named after Colin Minton Campbell, Chairman 1874-83. Built at Stoke in 1882, it was one of only three named NSR locomotives. *IAL/Bucknall Collection*

Left: Among a number of designs on the NSR were two saddle tanks, built at Stoke in 1881. Both were used for training footplatemen. *IAL/Bucknall Collection*

Below left: Company policy was to acquire locomotives in small batches, either building them at Stoke or ordering from private contractors. No 33 was among a number of 0-6-0Ts built at Stoke in 1883. *IAL/Bucknall Collection*

Left: 'Dressed over-all' for Queen Victoria's Diamond Jubilee in 1897. This Class A tank No 35, was built at Stoke in 1881. *LGRP*

Below left: No 35 pictured as rebuilt in 1898 as a neat 2-4-2T. It is seen at Stoke in 1913. *IAL/Bucknall Collection*

Above right: Class B 2-4-0T No 48 was one of five built at Stoke in 1887 to handle growing passenger traffic on the Loop line. *LPC*

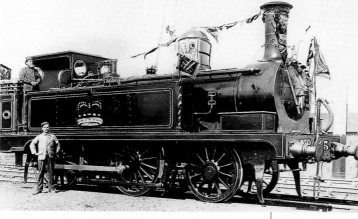

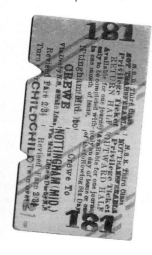

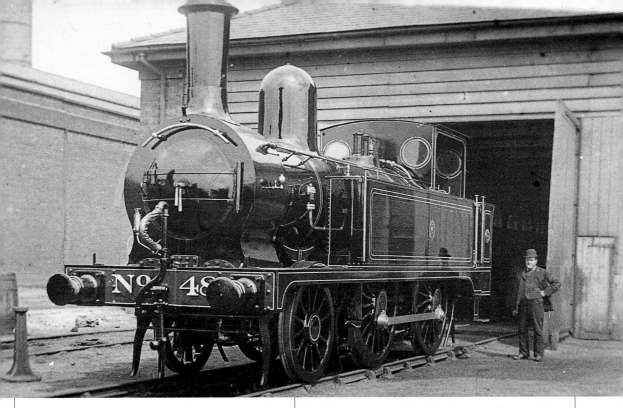

general design of the company's locomotives after John Henry Adams became Locomotive Superintendent in 1902. In 1906, he built two 2-4-0s which were the last of several thousand 2-4-0 tender engines built in Britain. While the NSR used them on most of its express services, 2-4-0Ts handled short distance passenger trains. They were also worked by 0-6-2Ts and a number of 0-6-4Ts, allocated to heavy goods traffic after their driving wheels were found to be too small for maintaining passenger schedules, for which they had been designed.

In 1907, Adams introduced the 'M' class 0-4-4Ts, adapted from the highly successful 'L' class 0-6-2Ts, built by Vulcan Foundry in 1903. For the bogies, Adams chose a well-known type designed by his father, well able to master the tight curves of the Loop line.

The four 4-4-0s which Adams designed for the North Wales expresses won the approval of LNWR staff at Llandudno Junction, where they were serviced. LNWR men admired the footplate with the NSR's traditional right-hand controls — opposite to Crewe practice. The LNWR staff thought the wheels too small for really fast running, but that mattered little as the NSR had nothing to match the generous layout of the Chester & Holyhead main line. But despite their small wheels, the NSR 4-4-0s maintained a 62min booking over the 62½ miles between Crewe and Rhyl.

When steam railmotors were needed for local services in the Stoke area in 1905, three were bought from Beyer Peacock. They were basically the maker's design with horizontal outside cylinders mounted between the axles, driving forward on the leading wheels. Two innovations were outside Walschaerts valve gear and Belpaire fireboxes. The whole engine was housed in a cab-style structure with only the smokebox and chimney protruding.

They were designed to run at 20mph on gradients as stiff as 1 in 60, but they were soon found inadequate, partly because they could not pull a trailer coach. Even as single units, they were unsatisfactory on the Loop and other services. They were restricted to the Stoke to Newcastle-under-Lyme link before being stored out of use.

There was always something to interest the NSR locomotive enthusiast, with Stoke producing a host of different designs or modifying earlier types. In 1908-9, a batch of 0-6-2Ts had cab roofs different from those which the company had ordered from the Vulcan Foundry five years earlier. They also had higher bunkers. Eight tanks, classed 'New L', were the first built under a new policy of building locomotives in batches of four or eight.

The final Stoke designs were the work of J. A. Hookham, Works Manager since 1902, who was promoted on the death of Adams in 1915. Innovation continued despite World War 1 and in 1917 he designed, with the company's electrical engineer A. F. Rock, a small, four-wheel, battery electric locomotive for shunting at Oakamoor Copper Works. It is now preserved.

Another of Hookham's unusual designs was an experimental four-cylinder tank engine, the only one of its type to run in Britain. Designed for quick acceleration with local trains, it was not a success and in 1924 it was converted to an 0-6-0 goods tender engine.

The NSR was not the only locomotive builder in Stoke: some 1,500 were built at the California Works of Kerr Stuart & Co between 1892 and 1930, when the firm went out of business. The works lay between the Trent & Mersey Canal and the NSR main line, between Whieldon Road Halt and Mount Pleasant Halt, the latter built to serve them. Two Kerr Stuart locomotives were bought by the NSR in 1910: 0-6-0Ts, originally destined for South America, but never delivered.

Stoke was also the headquarters of the NSR Locomotive, Carriage & Wagon Department, which employed 750 men and where premium pupils learned their trade. In late Victorian days, a five year apprenticeship included a year in the drawing office and spells in the running department, firing goods engines and working with the breakdown gang.

Stoke locomotive allocations were a spotter's dream, with virtually all types and most of the fleet being shedded there. The allocation of 125 was 110 more than that of Alsager, the second biggest shed. The third in size, Macclesfield, had 12 locomotives, while Derby, Uttoxeter, Burton and Crewe sheds had less than 10 each. Sub-sheds at Market Drayton and Leek Brook each had two locomotives. The NSR kept its own engines at the LNWR sheds at Manchester Longsight, Liverpool Edge Hill and Stafford, and on the Midland at Wellingborough.

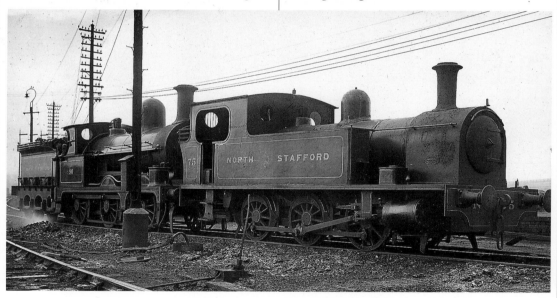

Above: With an extended smokebox, 0-6-0T No 75 was perhaps the ugliest of the locomotive fleet. It was one of two built for the Argentine Railways by Kerr Stuart in 1919, but never delivered and sold instead to the NSR. *IAL/Bucknall Collection*

Left: Four-cylinder 0-6-0T No 23 was the last design of J. A. Hookham, the last Locomotive Superintendent, who was in office from 1915-22. *IAL/Bucknall Collection*

Right: Breaktime at Stoke Works with workers grouped round a large heating stove; bowler-hatted foreman in the centre. Men climbed a long ladder to reach safety valves. *Author's Collection*

Centre right: Class 100 0-6-0 No 100 outside its birthplace, Stoke Works, in 1896. The coupling rods are painted white. *Author's Collection*

Below: Unsuccessful as a tank, No 23 was converted into a tender locomotive and taken into LMS stock as No 2367. It was scrapped in 1928. *LPC*

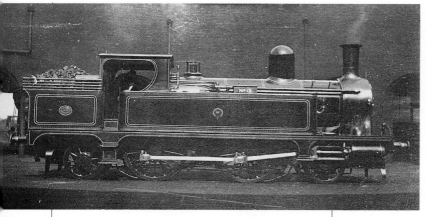

Left: Class 9 2-4-2T No 12 (as shown on a plate above the tank), in its final form after rebuilding from a 2-4-0T. It is pictured in Stoke roundhouse, which had an open-air turntable. Stoke's final NSR allocation was of 125 locomotives, mostly stabled in a new straight shed on the opposite (up) side of the main line. *Author's Collection*

Above: The 1910 scene at the straight shed, with a Class G 4-4-0, built that year, and Class D 0-6-0T No 57. On the right is the bunker of Class M 0-4-4T No 9. *IAL/Bucknall Collection*

Left: Stoke Shed 1925: LMS 0-6-0 No 2320, ex-NSR Class E No 74 and ex-NSR 'New C' 0-6-4T No 5 (LMS No 2047) in the foreground. Both of the ex-NSR locomotives survived until 1934. *LGRP*

Passenger rolling stock

An LNWR express including first class diners and saloons calling at Stoke must have been viewed with envy by workers waiting on draughty platforms for NSR Loop and other local services, generally made up of short rakes of four-wheel, four-compartment coaches. The NSR offered little comfort to working class passengers.

In winter 1849, the NSR board decreed that passenger trains should be made up of first and second class covered carriages and open thirds. But when winter set in, rebuilding began of open carriages, after it was laid down that Parliamentary trains had to have covered accommodation. The conversion programme took three years.

Guards sat on carriage roofs, riding with passenger baggage carried under waterproof covers, which had to be pulled back and then replaced at most stations.

After dark, Victorian passengers could easily find the class of accommodation they had booked by seeing how well they were lit. First class compartments were the most welcoming, brightly lit by four oil lamps. Second class coaches had two lamps, while in third class stock, one lamp placed above a shoulder-high partition dimly lit two compartments.

Coach design improvements were often dictated by higher running speeds and the practices of surrounding companies. The bell and external communication system was adopted late in 1860 for fitting to trains running over the LNWR, which already had the system. Brake vans became more common, although rule books of the mid-1860s still warned guards that they had to be sure that passengers' luggage was properly stacked on carriage roofs. The communication cord was fitted to stock of through services from summer 1869, and also the simple vacuum brake, as used on the LNWR, although that was not widely introduced by the NSR until 14 years later, providing a measure of the slow pace of change.

By the time Queen Victoria died, the NSR had begun installing electric light in carriages. It was the largest of only three British companies that switched directly from oil to electric, by-passing

Right: Life after NSR: a four-wheel composite coach with one first class and three third class compartments, in a dilapidated condition at Kinnerley on the Shropshire & Montgomeryshire Light Railway in 1935.
Photomatic Ltd

Below: Third class saloon No 143, built at Stoke in 1909, had a large 48-seater saloon and lavatory compartment. It survived until withdrawal by the LMS in 1937.
'Manifold' Collection

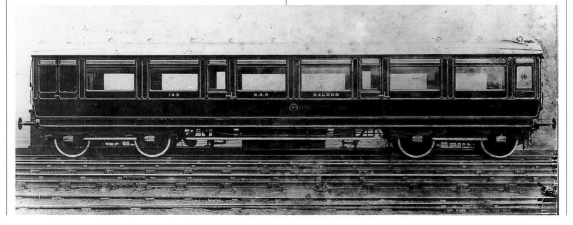

gas systems. The system pioneered by the NSR was initially far from perfect. The first sets were powered by a crated battery housed in the guard's van, but dynamos were primitive and the lights went out when speed fell below 10mph.

Conversion was slow and some of the 500 coaches were still oil lit in 1910 — 17 years after the experiment began.

Gradually, the length of coaches was increased, but four- and six-wheel stock formed virtually the whole of that in use up to Grouping. Bogie coaches were built from 1906 for the Llandudno services in summer and Derby-Crewe in winter. Measuring 52ft 6in over buffers, they were the company's longest vehicles and the most comfortable. Many were built at Stoke, but some were ordered from private contractors.

Although virtually all coaches had been equipped with steam heating by the end of World War 1, there was none installed in 13 veteran four-wheel coaches, in which miners travelled to and from work.

Goods rolling stock

At Grouping, the LMS acquired 6,612 NSR goods vehicles, of which more than 5,000 were wooden-bodied goods and mineral trucks. There were also more than 300 covered wagons — some fitted for silk traffic from Leek, Macclesfield and Congleton — 200 rail and timber trucks, a similar number of locomotive coal wagons, 130 goods brake vans, 66 cattle trucks, 53 milk vans and 360 service vehicles.

Such figures fail to reflect the tremendous volume of goods traffic worked over the system, for far larger than the entire NSR wagon fleet was the combined total of private owner wagons handled in the Potteries. Most pits, ironworks, coal, coke and patent fuel plants, and other industrial undertakings, had their own rolling stock, as did distributive traders.

NSR brake vans were distinctive with half boxed-in verandahs and a small window in the side. Most unusual and a familiar sight for years, were animal vans specially built for Barnum & Bailey's Circus, which had its central English depot at Cliff Vale, Stoke.

Considering its close ties with the LNWR, it was perhaps surprising that the NSR loading gauge was slightly more restrictive, allowing for van widths six inches less than standard on many company lines.

Left: Oil-lit six-wheel invalid and family saloon No 83 in the livery used by the NSR until 1896. Note the white-rimmed wheels. *LGRP*

Right: The volume of milk traffic handled by the NSR from farms in rural areas surrounding the Potteries was reflected in an order for six milk vans to carry traffic far beyond North Staffordshire. They were delivered in 1911 by the Metropolitan C&W Co. *HMRS Collection*

Lower right: Wooden 10-ton covered wagons were a familiar sight in many goods trains in the Potteries. No 5427 was among an order of 50 built by Metropolitan C&W in 1912. *HMRS Collection*

Below left: Two 25-ton bogie well wagons were delivered by the Metropolitan C&W Co in 1921. No 4496 is illustrated. *HMRS Collection*

Right: The company's fleet of open wagons had mainly 2ft 3in sides built up of three planks. No 1800 was a 1912 product of the Birmingham Railway C&W Co. *HMRS Collection*

Below right: A display photograph of goods brake — spelt 'Break' — No 60, built by the Gloucester Wagon Co in 1874. A feature of all the company's brake vans was a half boxed-in veranda end and a small side window. *HMRS Collection*

Stations
and Signalboxes

From the earliest days, the company was noted for the imaginative architecture of its stations. They immediately won approval from writers like Charles Knight, who reported on main line stations in 1848. He found Etruria small and insignificant and Burslem (later Longport) just a little better.

Above left: The LMS allowed local trains, including Loop line services, 10 minutes for non-stop runs over the 5³/₄ miles from Uttoxeter to Leigh. *LGRP*

Below left: For all its magnificence, Trentham Park had only a short life from 1910 until closure of the short branch in 1964 – seven years after the last excursion train ran. *Real Photos*

Below: Keele station, pictured in 1952, was situated on the Market Drayton-Stoke line. To the west of the station there was the junction for the line towards Audley. *LGRP*

'Lane End is better still; but Stoke is really magnificent. It is the centre of the company's operations — their offices, engine-houses, depots, workshops and warehouses; and it certainly indicates that the Directors have sanguine anticipations of a large future traffic. We hope, for the sake of the Company and the district, that such will prove the case. The works of the station show a plan of great beauty and magnitude. The railway is four lines in width at this spot; and the booking offices and arrival and departure platforms lie on both sides to accommodate the up and down traffic. The whole of the appointments have a completeness and a high finish which we are accustomed to look for only at the great terminal stations.'

Many improvements were made at Stoke through the years. The present overall roof dates from 1893-4 when the station was virtually rebuilt and electric lighting installed, fed by the company's

own power station adjacent to a subway. The last major improvement carried out by the company was to open out the entrance from the spacious booking hall to the platforms through an arch in memory of workers killed in World War 1.

Several other notable stations which also survive as listed buildings are in the Churnet Valley. They were the work of Pugin, the noted Victorian architect, who also partly designed Alton Towers, seat of the Earl of Shrewsbury.

Yet not all of the NSR's passengers began or ended journeys at stations of striking designs. Whether they attracted people to travel by train is debateable, because some of the best were built in small towns and other country areas where passengers were few and train services scant. On the busiest routes, including the Loop, most stations were functional and basic, with narrow platforms which were uncomfortable when they were crowded, and few facilities. Passengers often complained about many of them.

There were about 150 signalboxes at Grouping. The NSR shared with the London Brighton & South Coast the distinction of being the first British railways to complete interlocking (of points with signals) on all passenger lines. The work was completed in 1880, well ahead of most companies.

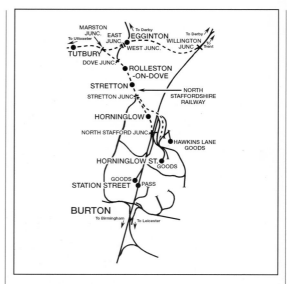

Above: Burton on Trent was a source of lucrative traffic for the NSR despite intense competition.

Below: Despite having only wooden buildings, Kidsgrove station had an ornate entrance. Note early postwar cars parked outside in 1952. *LGRP*

Above right: Tunstall was the terminus of some Loop line services, which used a cross over at the far end of the platform. *LGRP*

Below left: Fenton with platform canopies of distinctive style as seen in 1952. *LGRP*

Below: Clifton Yard, one of four boxes on the Rocester to Ashbourne branch. The NSR had three standard designs of signalcabins: McKenzie & Holland to 1876 when the NSR introduced its own design. A second and more numerous type was built from 1885 to Grouping. *H. B. Oliver*

CLIFTON YARD

Left: Longport station box, controlling a busy crossing of the main line, was open continuously. *J. A. Peden*

Below: The NSR used the standard slender-arm signals of its contractors, McKenzie & Holland of Worcester. Older types had a tall spike on a fluted umbrella finial. Later signals had a plain ball and spike. *Both LGRP*

Below: Leek was an example of a market town where the goods yard was still busy several years after regular local passenger services had been withdrawn. No 75037 shunts the yard in April 1966. *Geoffrey Brown*

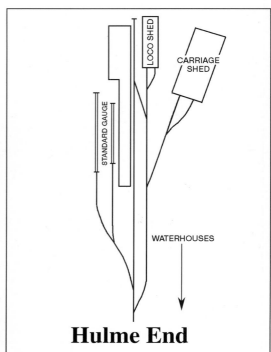

Left: Steeply sloping roofs and small entrance porches were among distinctive features of many NSR signal boxes. Their names were shown on cast metal plates. *IAL*

Hulme End

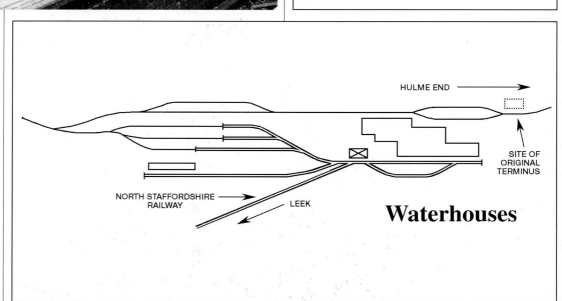

Waterhouses

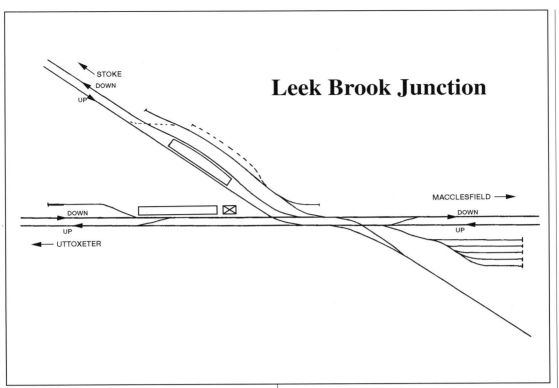

Leek Brook Junction

STOKE

DOWN

UP

MACCLESFIELD →

DOWN

UP

DOWN

UP

← UTTOXETER

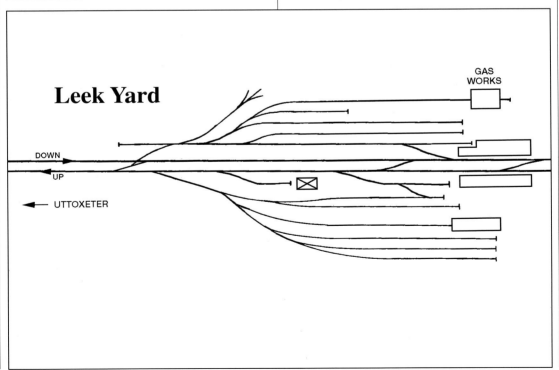

Leek Yard

GAS
WORKS

DOWN

UP

← UTTOXETER

Cold Meece

28 JUNE 1958

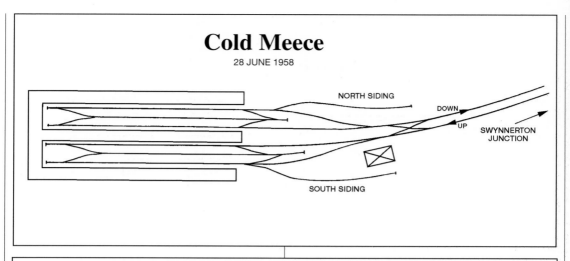

NORTH SIDING

DOWN

UP

SWYNNERTON
JUNCTION

SOUTH SIDING

Stone Junction

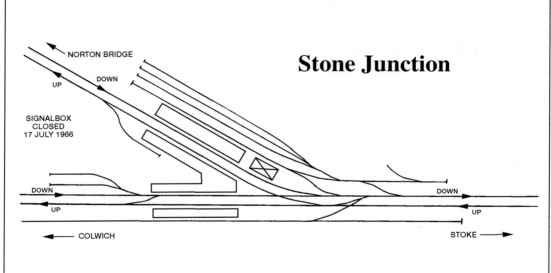

NORTON BRIDGE

UP

DOWN

SIGNALBOX
CLOSED
17 JULY 1966

DOWN

UP

DOWN

UP

COLWICH

STOKE

Silverdale

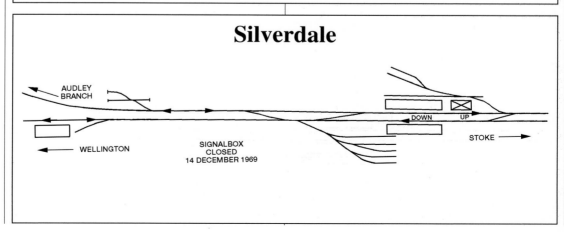

AUDLEY
BRANCH

DOWN

UP

STOKE

WELLINGTON

SIGNALBOX
CLOSED
14 DECEMBER 1969

Cheadle (Staffs)

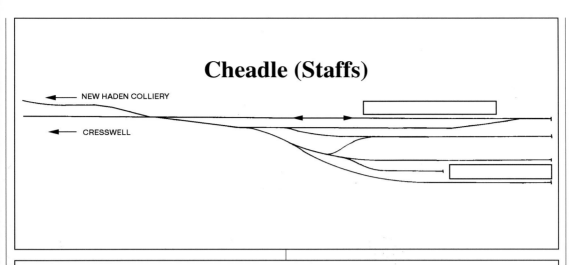

Kidsgrove Central Junction

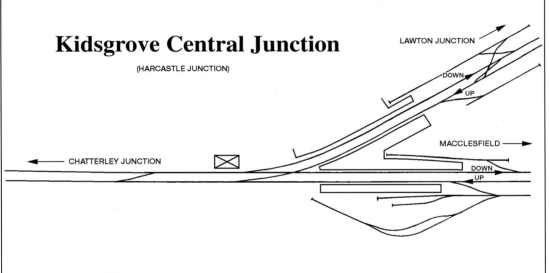

Congleton

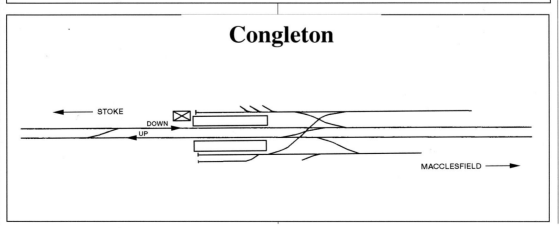

London Midland & Scottish Years

Grouping robbed the Potteries of a railway which many local people regarded as their own — a mood reflected in the dedication by the Manifold group of historians in their history of the NSR, published in 1952: 'To the immortal memory of the old "Knotty" and all its railwaymen who by their devotion to duty earned the North Stafford such a high reputation among our railways.'

In national terms, the NSR passed into the LMS as the 17th biggest company assessed by locomotive ownership and the 19th in mileage. The Macclesfield, Bollington & Marple Line passed to the joint control of the LMS and LNER. The LMS inherited the Trent & Mersey Canal and the NSR hotels. It also took over the Caldon quarry, but that remained profitable only until 1925 because of closure of the Brunner Mond works at Sandbach five years earlier. The quarry was leased to a Sheffield company in 1934.

The biggest of the LMS economies was the 1926-7 closure of Stoke Locomotive Works, perhaps inevitable because of those at Crewe and Derby being so close. But the LMS cushioned the effect on employment in the Potteries by transferring many men there and opening a halt inside Crewe works for workmen's services to and from the Potteries.

Other economies sealed the fate of a number of short distance, little used, branch passenger services. The earliest casualties were railmotor halts at Brampton and Sideway in 1923-4. Another two — Knutton and Hartshill & Basford — followed in 1927. This was the year which brought the first branch closure, regular passenger trains ceasing on the Biddulph Valley line from 11 July. It was a busy mineral line considered to have little passenger potential, a fact confirmed by the closure of a large ironworks the following year. The NSR had run four weekday trains, allowed 50min to cover the 14 miles on the roundabout route from Stoke to Congleton. They made seven intermediate stops at stations and halts, all but two on the Biddulph Valley section.

Above left: Ex-NSR 'New C' 0-6-4T No 54, now LMS No 2042, prepares to leave Stoke with a southbound service in 1931. *LGRP*

Below left: The Knotty atmosphere lingered for years after Grouping and it was not until 1928-9 that their ranks were severely depleted by the withdrawal of 51 locomotives. Subsequent scrappings averaged 10 a year. In 1931, former Class M 0-4-4T No 9 (LMS No 1431) is seen at Stoke North with mixed LMS stock. *LGRP*

Below: After Grouping, five class B 2-4-0Ts were switched from NSR local services to those of the North London line. Former NSR No 7, LMS No 1451, is seen here at Poplar in January 1927. *H. C. Casserley*

Left: 0-4-4T LMS No 1431 was not withdrawn until 1936. It is at Leek in summer 1933 with a Churnet Valley local service composed of LMS carriages. *H. C. Casserley*

Centre left: A stopping service departing Stoke in spring 1932, headed by ex-NSR 0-6-2T No 89 of 1913. Its LMS number is in tall numerals on the bunker, well stacked with coal. *H. C. Casserley*

Below left: LMS compound 4-4-0s gradually replaced NSR 4-4-0s on main line services. No 1117 is caught is caught at Uttoxeter in spring 1932.
Dr J. R. Hollick

The Trentham Park branch lost its local passenger service from Stoke in 1927 but was retained for excursions, and in 1939 still had a separate entry in Bradshaw with a table headed 'Stoke-on-Trent-Trentham-Trentham Park: Sundays only.' Timing columns were blank. The branch terminus was renamed Trentham Gardens in autumn 1946.

A summer 1930 casualty was the passenger service on the Kidsgrove-Sandbach branch. It had seen one of the first changes under the LMS regime, Wheelock & Sandbach being renamed Sandbach (Wheelock) in April 1923.

Spring 1931 saw the withdrawal of Audley branch passenger services, which was a precursor for economies on the Stoke-Market Drayton line, with the closure of Madeley Road station (within sight of the West Coast main line) and the singling in October 1934 of almost seven miles between Silverdale and Pipe Gate. It created the longest single block system on what had been the NSR.

In 1933 two miles of the Cheadle branch were diverted because of a troublesome tunnel. Far more widely publicised was closure of the heavily loss-making Leek & Manifold Valley Light Railway in March 1934. Later the LMS donated the trackbed to Staffordshire County Council, which turned it into a footpath. A section was converted into a road in 1953. After the narrow gauge shut down, passenger services to Waterhouses were withdrawn in 1935.

Two economies made between the end of World War 2 and Nationalisation were the closure of country stations between Stone and Colwich in January 1947 and of the Jamage branch at the end of the year, after two local pits ceased production.

First stop for some local services between Stoke and Stafford today is Wedgwood, four miles south of Stoke, a wartime halt opened beside the pottery factory on 1 January 1940. Far more significant was the construction of the double-track Cold Meece branch, opened off the Stone-Norton Bridge line in August 1941. More than three million passengers a year — an average of 8,000 a day — travelled to and from stations all over the Potteries on services that never appeared in timetables because of secrecy surrounding a large Royal Ordnance factory built at Swynnerton. Close by was an American Air Force base which thousands of personnel reached by train. The Cold Meece branch was closed by BR in summer 1958. It never carried freight, as this was handled at Badnall Wharf on the Crewe-Stafford main line.

Another large Royal Ordnance factory at Radway Green, east of Crewe, was served by a platform called Millway, opened by the LMS in October 1944. Again, it was not shown in public timetables.

The LMS made few changes to the basic pattern of NSR passenger services, but there were radical alterations in motive power and timings of Euston-Manchester expresses via Stoke. Despite hopes in the Potteries that Grouping would bring faster links with the Capital, it was not until 1925 that Euston-Stoke services even returned to 1914 timings.

Almost immediately after Grouping, 4-4-0s — ex-LNWR and Midland compounds — were introduced on Euston expresses, but they were soon displaced by 'Claughton' class 4-6-0s. They were used until the introduction of 'Jubilee' class 4-6-0s, which were an instant success.

Because of weight restrictions on the Congleton viaducts, the original 'Royal Scot' 4-6-0s were barred from the Potteries. Rebuilt 'Royal Scots' were allowed, but they were not as successful as the 'Jubilees'.

The weight and speed restrictions prevented the Potteries from benefitting fully from express service improvements initiated by the LMS in 1927. A year later, North Staffordshire acquired its first named train when the noon express — the former 12.10pm Manchester departure — became the 'Lancastrian'.

It achieved fame among enthusiasts as an express which, when traffic was heavy, was run in separate portions over separate routes through the Potteries. A portion from Colne in northeast Lancashire was routed through the Churnet Valley, rather than being attached to the main express at Stockport.

The title was also bestowed on the 6pm Euston departure for Manchester but it ran via Crewe, hauled by 'Royal Scots' and, later, Stanier Pacifics, running nonstop on mile-a-minute timings to Wilmslow, 21 miles closer to Manchester than Stoke.

The heaviest locomotives allowed on the up 'Lancastrian' were 'Patriot' and 'Jubilee' 4-6-0s, and inevitably they were banked from Macclesfield to the Moss box. South of Stoke, they maintained 60mph timings via Colwich and reached Euston 20min quicker than in NSR days.

The express made a late-afternoon arrival at Euston at 3.40pm. That was only half an hour before the departure of the main evening express for the Potteries — the down 'Mancunian'. Besides Stoke, it called at Congleton, not served by the up 'Lancastrian', and Macclesfield. Like the 'Lancastrian', the 'Mancunian' ran only one way through Stoke, the morning up service being routed via Crewe.

After Grouping, the Potteries remained an area through which only Manchester-Stoke-London passengers could travel at speed. This was mainly due to the large number of stops that local

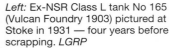

Left: Ex-NSR Class L tank No 165 (Vulcan Foundry 1903) pictured at Stoke in 1931 — four years before scrapping. *LGRP*

Below left: After Grouping, ex-NSR locomotives continued to work in the Manchester district. In 1936, ex-NSR tank No 1 of the 'New L' class, built at Stoke 1923, was working at Longsight. It was carrying a 9B Stockport Edgeley shed plate. *LGRP*

Right: Cold Meece, a terminal never in public timetables, opened in summer 1941 to serve a large Royal Ordnance factory. In winter 1958, a 'Black Five' 4-6-0 departs with the 4.50pm workers' service to Newchapel. *H. B. Oliver*

services made on comparatively short journeys. In 1897, the 10.10am from Stafford to Manchester London Road took 40min to Stoke and reached Macclesfield at 11.55am, where passengers had to change and wait 18min for the 7.30am Euston-Manchester express, booked at 20min over its final leg via Stockport.

A comparable 1947 service still took over two hours, the LMS maintaining the NSR practice of a protracted wait at Stoke. By 1947 it was shown in public timetables as 6min, 1min longer than in NSR days.

Crewe-Derby services never developed into the once-envisaged through route between northwest England and the Eastern Counties. Bradshaw's printed LMS timetables for Crewe-Derby linked to shorter distance services than those shown in

timetables of the NSR, which linked them to LNWR Anglo-Scottish West Coast services and Midland and GNR expresses between Derby and London. Connections shown with LMS Crewe-Derby services were restricted to those to and from Blackpool, the North Wales coast and the Midland main line between Derby and St Pancras.

In 1897, the 11am Crewe-Derby service took 2hr 8min for the 51 miles with 15 stops. Half a century later, a comparable service took only 10min less.

Loop line boundaries were extended to embrace Uttoxeter and Congleton, rather than Blythe Bridge and Longton to Kidsgrove. The 'Loop line' title was dropped in LMS timetables, which showed more than 20 weekday trains each way.

Goods services and depots

The NSR often boasted of having more than 200 miles of running powers over the lines of rival companies, but similar facilities which those companies received in return led to fierce competition for goods traffic in the Potteries. The LNWR and Midland built their own goods depots in the four main towns, although some were not even rail connected.

When that competition ended with Grouping, the LMS quickly began concentrating goods traffic at single depots in Stoke, Hanley, Longport for Burslem, Longton for Fenton, Tunstall and Newcastle. All the depots were within a four-mile radius of Stoke, which gradually became the main centre for miscellaneous sundries traffic and much of the traffic destined for the other depots was transhipped from there.

Locomotives and rolling stock

In a paperback, quite lavish for its day, *Locomotives of the LMS Past & Present*, which the company published in 1930, only two NSR locomotives were classed among principal LMS locomotive types: 4-4-2T No 2180 and 0-6-4T No 2048.

By then, many ex-NSR locomotives in their prime had been scrapped under the LMS policy of standardisation, because it did not consider the maintenance of small classes economic. More than 50 were withdrawn in 1928-9. At least 10 engines a year were withdrawn, until only two were left in LMS stock by the end of 1937.

A number had spent their final years elsewhere on the LMS, including five 2-4-0Ts which worked on the North London section. Some tank locomotives went to collieries; five 'New L' class 0-6-2Ts received a well-publicised retirement at Bridgewater Collieries Railway near Manchester. One of them was subsequently preserved.

Also preserved is one engine which remained in LMS service stock: a small battery electric shunter

now numbered BEL 2, which worked at Bolton's Sidings, Oakamoor, until its withdrawal in 1964.

The LMS 'restocked' the old NSR with locomotives more powerful than those they replaced. From 1926 the LMS sent new '4F' 0-6-0s to the Potteries and subsequent arrivals included 'George V' class 4-4-0s and 4-6-0 'Experiments', ex-LNWR 0-8-0s, new Fowler classes of 2-6-2 and 2-6-4 tanks and Mogul 2-6-0s, 'Jinty' 0-6-0Ts and ageing Lancashire & Yorkshire and Midland tanks for shunting.

In the late 1930s, new Stanier designs began work, including his 2-6-2 and 2-6-4Ts, Class 5 mixed traffic and 'Jubilee' 4-6-0s.

Gradually, there were economies in the former NSR shed organisation, beginning in 1926 when Stoke and other depots were all given the number 40, which they retained for seven years until a further reorganisation brought the introduction of numbers and letters for depots. Three sheds were included in the Crewe district: Stoke (5D), Alsager (5E) and Uttoxeter (5F). Macclesfield (9C) went under the Manchester Longsight district. The NSR sheds at Crewe, Burton and Colwick closed soon after Grouping and their small allocations of locomotives were transferred to LNWR sheds.

Later economies were at Market Drayton, where the shed closed in 1931, as did those of Leek Brook and Ashbourne the following year.

Coaching stock

Equally drastic as locomotive withdrawals were those of coaches, although many were far older than the locomotives. All four-wheel coaches were quickly withdrawn and in the first decade of Grouping, one third of NSR coaching stock was withdrawn. Mainly it consisted of six-wheel coaches and vans built before 1901.

More modern bogie coaches survived through the LMS regime and into early BR days, until the arrival of DMUs. Several worked in the Furness district; others on the Southend line.

British Rail: Decades of Change

The atmosphere of the Knotty was swept away in an era of modernisation in the mid-1960s. Most radical changes came with 25kV electrification through the Potteries, which coincided with the final years of steam.

Local timetables got thinner as passenger services were withdrawn from a number of NSR branches between 1954-64. The same decade also saw the complete closure of a number of mineral-only branches.

The overhead electrification between Macclesfield-Stoke-Colwich and Stone-Norton Bridge was completed in 1967. This is now a far more important route than the former Crewe-Derby main line, which has lost most of its branches.

Euston-Manchester Piccadilly expresses running via Stoke and Macclesfield use the 2½-mile Harecastle Deviation, built to by-pass three ageing tunnels under the Trent and Mersey watershed. The £1 million project was carried out because the original tunnels had insufficient clearance for overhead lines and were in poor structural condition. It was estimated that civil engineers would have needed weekend possession for between 20 and 30 years to modernise them. To build the Deviation, which includes a 220yd tunnel, the alignments of the Chesterton branch and Chatterley sidings were altered. Both were later abandoned.

At Macclesfield, Hibel Road station was closed on 7 November 1960, coincident with the withdrawal of Churnet Valley passenger services to Leek, and replaced by Central which was extensively rebuilt. The project gave Macclesfield a single station, which it had wanted for nearly a century.

The Kidsgrove-Crewe section of the main line was not converted, partly because much of its traffic was freight to and from areas outside the Potteries, which had to be diesel hauled. And diesel was the only traction that could be used on Crewe-Derby passenger services.

At Crewe, the NSR up and down goods loops and the spur under the West Coast main line into Basford Hall sidings were among more than 70 miles of track within a mile of the station which were electrified.

Electrification work brought fresh life to the Market Drayton branch, with the opening in June 1962 of the Madeley Chord to the West Coast main line. It used an embankment constructed when the Market Drayton branch opened 90 years earlier but never developed as a link. During electrification, it was a diversionary route for traffic from Stoke and places south.

Above left: BR standard 'Clan' Pacific No 72005 *Clan Macgregor* at Blythe Bridge with the 1.40pm Llandudno-Derby on 8 August 1956. From the tall NSR box, signalmen had a commanding view of the level crossing. *Anthony Cox*

Left: Class 9F 2-10-0 No 92104 attacks the stiff gradient towards Fenton with a Derby line mineral working in 1966. A diesel locomotive giving banking assistance is passing Carter's Crossing signalbox. *M. G. Fell*

Right: A mineral working from Caldon arrives at Leek Brook, headed by an unidentified 'Black Five' 4-6-0 on 4 May 1964. *H. B. Oliver*

Left: Steam under the wires. Stoke is a station through which goods traffic has to pass. A 'Jinty' tank takes the middle up through road with a train of empty wagons, in August 1966. *M. G. Fell*

Below: Stoke 'long shed' was still busy in autumn 1966. Here the south end of the shed is viewed from the brake van of an RCTS railtour. *M. G. Fell*

Right: Class 9F 2-10-0s berthed alongside Stoke ash disposal and coaling plant of the 'long shed' shortly before closure in 1967. *M. G. Fell*

The Madeley-Apedale Junction section of the former Market Drayton branch remains open to serve a large colliery near Newcastle.

The Potteries electrification was completed after the West Coast main line. Electric services introduced from 2 January 1967 ran to steam timings until a switch was made to high speed services in the North Staffordshire and Birmingham areas on 6 March.

Most Euston-Manchester expresses of 1997 run via Stoke, which is a more profitable route than via Crewe, served by many West Coast expresses. Overall Euston-Manchester timings are about 2hr 30min, including 1hr 45min to Stoke; and another 16min from there to Macclesfield.

There are no intensive electrified local passenger services through the Potteries.

Although some stations were retained, they were little used, partly because Stoke station is a bus ride away from Hanley, the Potteries main and expanding shopping centre. Today, Central Trains maintain a Crewe-Nottingham service. DMUs take about 1hr 25min over the 50 miles from Crewe to Derby and 27min over the 16 miles to Nottingham, with four intermediate stops. In the 1980s, some of the DMU services were extended to Lincoln — 99¾ miles from Crewe.

There are still 10 main intermediate stations on the NSR section, including Tutbury & Hatton, reopened in 1989. Longport and Etruria are missed by a number of services, an economy initiated in summer 1979 when BR stated that the off-peak use of Etruria station was low. It reduced

the number of trains using the station to allow the slight acceleration of 'important Crewe-Derby cross-country services'.

Stoke remains the hub of the original 'scissors', though its role as a railway centre has declined in recent years, after enjoying one last bout of importance as headquarters of the Stoke-on-Trent Division of the London Midland Region. It was enlarged in 1966 to embrace North and Mid Wales from Holyhead to Aberystwyth (including BR's last steam railway, the narrow gauge Vale of Rheidol), and survived in that form until the Stoke, Manchester and Preston Divisions were merged into an enlarged Manchester Division in 1983.

The old NSR system attracted national interest when Britain's first automatic level-crossing half-barriers were installed at Spath, near Uttoxeter, in February 1961.

After electrification, others followed at Aston-by-Stone in 1967 and neighbouring Hixon, where 11 people, including three locomotive men, were killed and 45 people injured in a crash on 6 January 1968. A Manchester-Euston express hit a heavy road transporter carrying a transformer which was straddling the crossing. A formal inquiry was ordered under Section 7 of the Regulation of the Railways Act 1871. The section had been used only once before, following the Tay Bridge disaster of 1879. The Hixon Report placed blame in several quarters and called for basic changes in automatic crossing operation. The crossing had been converted to automatic under a British Railways Board Order which included in its title that of the 'North Staffordshire Railway'.

Passenger economies

Because of running mainly over short distances, former NSR train services were vulnerable to bus and car competition and a number of lines had been closed to passengers before the Beeching Report of March 1963.

Ashbourne lost its passenger services in November 1954 with the withdrawal of Uttoxeter-Buxton services, which supplemented a Uttoxeter local service. The route had been run down until, in the final years, there was a 4hr gap in the middle of the day in the local link to Ashbourne and a 7hr interval between Uttoxeter-Buxton through trains.

Stoke-Leek services succumbed to far more direct bus services in May 1956, although football specials continued for another four years. Also in May 1956, the Stoke-Market Drayton passenger service was cut back 12 miles to Silverdale. The Beeching Report was to recommend withdrawal of passenger services over the 4¼-mile stub between Stoke, Newcastle and Silverdale.

By 1950, Sunday trains had been withdrawn and the weekday service reduced to seven each way, including three Silverdale-Stoke trains which carried through coaches for Birmingham New Street.

The Trentham Gardens branch stopped handling excursions in autumn 1957 and was finally closed. The Cold Meece branch followed nearly a year later and Millway, serving Radway Green ROF, closed in January 1959. Tutbury-Burton local services ('Tutbury Jennie') ceased in June 1960, 11 years after the three intermediate branch stations had closed. Freight traffic continued until 1966.

A public inquiry preceded withdrawal of Churnet Valley regular passenger services on Bonfire Night 1960, when there was a rowdy farewell at Rudyard, once a quiet picnic spot.

Beeching listed for withdrawal the Loop line and Leek-Uttoxeter workmen's services. The specials ceased in January 1965, when Oakamoor Sand Sidings-Uttoxeter was closed completely.

The Loop line closed in March 1964, on the same day as Stoke-Silverdale passenger services. The Loop services had been ailing for years and DMUs, introduced seven years earlier, had failed to halt the decline in passengers.

The four mile branch from Cresswell to Cheadle — where some Loop line trains terminated — had closed to passengers in summer 1963, together with Tean Halt, the one intermediate call.

One of the last economies on lines with which the NSR was associated was the complete closure in January 1970 of the Macclesfield, Bollington & Marple Line between Macclesfield and Marple Rose Hill. The one-mile northern stub to Marple Wharf Junction still has a good passenger service to Manchester Piccadilly via Hyde (12½ miles). The MB&M was excluded from Labour's 'British Railways Network for Development' plan published in 1967, but the section to Rose Hill was reprieved because of extensive residential development.

Increased rail-road co-operation led to bus services appearing in BR passenger timetables. That, for the North Staffordshire lines of the London Midland Region for summer 1964, included a page detailing 'road-rail co-ordination'. Passengers were offered free bus vouchers if they arrived at Stafford or Crewe when there was no immediate train service forward to their destination in the Potteries.

The 1960s brought a steady decline in excursion traffic, which reached its annual peak during Stoke Wakes Weeks, when dozens of trains ran to seaside resorts, including Bournemouth and Scarborough, although Blackpool and North Wales remained the most popular destinations.

The Knotty enthusiast and author, Martin R. Connop Price, recalled that in 1961, 42 extra trains ran from the Potteries in the first of the Wakes Weeks, but only 11 in the second. Three years later, there were 28 additional trains on the first weekend and only seven on the second, yet it was estimated that up to 15,000 holiday-makers left North Staffordshire on the first day of the Wakes.

Locomotive shed, freight and depot changes

The rundown of steam caused closure of Stoke (code 5D), Alsager (5E) and Uttoxeter (5F) sheds. A total of 100 engines were allocated to Stoke straight shed and roundhouse. Both closed in 1967, when the roundhouse began falling into dereliction before its demolition in winter 1973. Alsager shed had closed in 1962 and Uttoxeter in 1964.

A freight terminal opened at Stoke in spring 1961. It was the first purpose-built concentration depot under a major London Midland Region freight traffic plan to streamline and speed up traffic handling. It replaced the NSR Stoke goods depot and eight others, all in the Potteries with the exception of Stafford.

When the Stoke Division was formed, there was still heavy and varied freight traffic originating in the Potteries. Generally, the withdrawal of goods services was slower than that of passengers.

The Macclesfield, Bollington & Marple was one of the few local lines on which passenger and goods traffic was withdrawn simultaneously and the line closed completely. Most lines in the industrial areas once served by the NSR retained freight services for some years after passenger services had ceased. Goods trains could still be seen at Ashbourne a decade after passenger trains, and on the western end of the Stoke-Market Drayton branch freight services outlived those for passengers by 11 years.

The Biddulph Valley branch, closed to passengers in 1927, stayed open for goods until 1968 while the Sandbach branch, closed to passengers in 1930, was officially a freight line until 1971.

Some of the largest volumes of traffic were from quarries east of Stoke, including Caldon Low. The heavily-graded Leek Brook-Caldon Low line was mothballed in February 1989. Five years later the quarry was reached by the Branch Line Society Caldon Peak railtour.

After BR lost a contract to carry industrial sand to Merseyside, more than 20 miles of railway was closed and also mothballed until complete closure in May 1993. The section stretched from Stoke to Leek Brook and eight miles south through the Churnet Valley to Oakamoor.

The section includes Cheddleton, now the headquarters of the Churnet Valley Railway, a preservation society which has bought seven miles of trackbed to exploit a 'superbly picturesque route' as part of North Staffordshire's heritage.

A less ambitious though pleasant stretch of line which occupies part of the Churnet trackbed north of Leek, is that of a narrow gauge line based at Rudyard, close to the lake.

Another notable standard gauge preserved steam line, which keeps alive the industrial atmosphere which was so strong among lines in the Potteries, is the Foxfield Light Railway, established in 1967. It uses some three miles of an 1893 industrial line between Foxfield Colliery and the NSR at Dilhorne, near Blythe Bridge. All its locomotives worked at industrial sites, including mines, gasworks and collieries.

Right: Stoke long shed, May 1965, with a varied array of ex-LMS and BR standard classes. *N. Fields*

Below Right: Stoke roundhouse was also full of standard classes. The centre of the building, above the turntable, was open to the sky. *N. Fields*

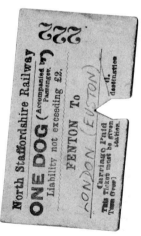

Right: A DMU comes off the Crewe branch at Kidsgrove and crosses the Trent & Mersey Canal. *R. W. Miller*

Routes and relics of the NSR are to be found in several sections of trackbed which have been developed into walkways. The Loop line Greenway, stretching from Hanley through Burslem to Tunstall, is among schemes which have helped rid the heart of the Potteries of its industrial image.

The Biddulph Valley Way utilises the trackbed as a recreation strip between Brunswick Wharf, Congleton, and the Cheshire boundary, as do the Salt Line, created from two sections of the Sandbach-Alsager branch, and the shorter Merelake Way, over part of the Audley branch from Alsager. Attractive colour leaflets have replaced Bradshaw as guides to some of these enterprises.

Finally, Stoke has a place in railway history as the penultimate home of the BR horse, for after the last one left for retirement in June 1964, only two remained at work at Newmarket.

Above: In summer 1967, diesel shunter No D4109 brings a loaded train off Parkhouse Colliery on the Chesterton branch. *M. G. Fell*

Below: Another preserved NSR locomotive is a battery-driven 0-4-0 built to work at Oakamoor in the Churnet Valley in 1917. It was photographed at Crewe in 1966 with a Class 86 electric locomotive then numbered E3183. *British Rail*